A WOMAN'S WAY TO
FREEDOM, POWER, LOVE, AND MAGIC

THE SOVEREIGNTY KNOT

MARISA GOUDY

Publishing Services provided by Paper Raven Books

Printed in the United States of America

First Printing, 2020

Paperback ISBN= 978-1-7341940-0-5
Hardback ISBN= 978-1-7341940-1-2

For my mother and the unbroken line of women who came before me. For my daughters and the women who may come after you.

And in memory of my Aunt Marian, who made this book possible. I wish I knew your story better.

Table of Contents

Foreword

I have had the joy and honor of witnessing some of Marisa Goudy's journey to the book you are holding in your hands. I have watched her dive deep into the tangle of the Sovereignty Knot, embrace its mystery, and bring its timeless teachings to life in her own life. I am pleased to report that she is as wise and witty, as humorous and humble on the page as she is in person. She is a woman who thinks in curves and leaps; she spins paradoxical ideas in the air as daringly as any juggler, word witch that she is. And it does take magic to translate a mercurial mind into a book with beautifully thought-out chapters, each one serving as guide and inspiration to the reader's own quest for Sovereignty.

The meditations in the book invite you to explore your inner terrain. As an experienced writing coach, Marisa provides prompts that will get the ink to flow or the keys to fly as you tell or retell the stories that illuminate your life. She also offers the inspired suggestion to create the map of your own Sovereign realm. This is a book that encourages you to be playful and serious, challenged and comforted.

Whatever else she is—guide, mentor, companion—Marisa is a superb and courageous storyteller. Always mindful that your story may be very different from hers, Marisa shares her personal stories as commingled princess, queen, and wise woman, daughter, mother, lover, rebel, nurturer, explorer, activist—in short, a woman losing and finding, claiming and reclaiming her Sovereign self. With great charm, she also retells ancient Irish stories and makes them accessible to those new to them, while offering fresh insights to those who know them well.

Find yourself a *shillelagh* (Irish walking stick), fill a knapsack with whatever you like best to eat and drink, tuck this book under your arm, and set out on a quest with no straight paths, just the assurance that each curve will lead you home to your Sovereign self.

Elizabeth Cunningham
Author of *The Maeve Chronicles* and other books

Acknowledgements

Since I have been writing this book in some shape or form since I was a myth-reading, goddess-seeking college student who said, "I want to write a book that someone like me needs to read," it's impossible to thank everyone who played a part in the creation of *The Sovereignty Knot*, but I'll give it a try…

Thanks to my aunt Maureen and cousin Alison for getting me back to Ireland after all these years, and to Niall, Jason, Ruaidhrí, and Mairéad for making it feel like old times.

This book was birthed into the world thanks to the support of longtime and recent mentors. Elizabeth Cunningham's practical, compassionate wisdom and magical, fictional world have been a continuing source of inspiration. Kristoffer "KC" Carter of This Epic Life helped me figure out what it means to "Be Sovereign Everywhere." Eleanora Amendolara has been my "spiritual mom" and my most important teacher for well over a decade. I'm also grateful to my fellow students at the Sacred Center for the Healing Arts and all we've learned together over the years.

My deepest thanks to my Noelle Adamo, who has been a dear friend since the days of that basement apartment, for reading my earliest draft. Having Dawn Goforth-Kelly, Jennifer Jines, and my favorite high school English teacher, Patricia Lawrence, read along as I polished each chapter meant the world to me. I'm so fortunate to have had the support of Morgan MacDonald and the rest of the Paper Raven Books team throughout the writing and publishing process and I'm so thankful for their insight and expertise. Kate Chadbourne of The Bardic Academy (and my first Irish language instructor at Boston College way back in 1997) helped me across the finish line. I am deeply grateful for her insightful comments, particularly about Brigid, the Cailleach, and my presentation of Irish myth.

The continuing dedication and companionship of the members of the Sovereign Writers Circle have been the best things this writer and writing coach could ask for. I'm so grateful to all of my clients who cared about this book through its development, especially those who took part in Your Sovereign Awakening, the program where I tested much of this material.

And I am grateful to my family and the friends who are like family. Knowing that Michelle Wolin was there to love my daughters and say "I hear you, Mama" when I was having all the feelings at preschool drop-off means everything to me. Kerri McIntyre, I couldn't have written this book if you weren't always just a text away and fully able to understand the other meaning of "SK." Jessica Savage, you know the princess in me better than anyone and I know you were with me in spirit as I wrote this book. Thanks to my dad, and all the Glasers. I'm so lucky to have a clan like you! Moira and Mairead, thank you for being such magical fairy souls and for giving me so many chances to walk the Sovereignty talk. Thank you for trying to understand, "Please, Mommy just needs to finish one more page." I love you and your daddy, too. You're a star, Bear. Thank you for being the earth so I could be the air.

Fáilte

Fáilte is a word from the Irish language that is etched into the glass doors of pubs from Dublin to Boston. It is stitched into needlepoint samplers hung on kitchen walls in small towns and big cities around the world. Its meaning is simple and pure: *Welcome.*

Welcome to *The Sovereignty Knot: A Woman's Way to Freedom, Power, Love, and Magic.*

Together, we're going to explore the beauty, possibility, pain, and contradictions that are inherent to the modern woman's experience. This book is about recognizing your own power and leading with your own magic. It's also about strengthening your connections with the people you love and being of service in the world.

In these pages, you're invited to lose yourself in stories both old and new. More importantly, you're invited to uncover and write your own stories based on the ideas you find within.

To enter the Sovereignty Knot means you're ready to look closely at both the beautiful patterns and the terrible tangles of life. *How can you maintain your individuality while living in community? How can you find personal, creative, and spiritual freedom when you're constantly navigating your relationships with others? How can you stand Sovereign in your own power and contribute to the greater good?*

These questions can snarl you up, but these tensions also make up the very fabric of life. The answers can help you unlock your sense of meaning and purpose and bring more passion and wonder into your life. This book offers the inspiration and support to explore such territory because, even if Sovereignty is an inside job, you never have to do it all alone.

Women everywhere are seeking to live Sovereign lives. You just need to know where to look.

Begin by pushing open a door that reads *"fáilte."*

Imagine you're entering a cozy room. There's a hum of gentle conversation and music that makes you tap your toes. Occasional gales of laughter rise above the sweet din. There's a circle around the fireplace, and it expands to make room for you. Someone puts a glass in your hand. It's full of whatever you like to drink in the presence of good company—tea, whiskey, beer, you choose. Getting comfortable now, you look around and realize that this is a circle of women. Perfectly imperfect women like you. Daughters, mothers, grandmothers. Warriors, artists, and sorceresses, too.

One voice in particular bids you welcome. You're greeted by an American woman with red hair, green eyes, and a broad smile. I introduce myself as this book's author and your guide along this path to Sovereignty. I'm also a longtime student of Irish myth and Celtic spirituality, as well as a storyteller, an energy healer, a tarot reader, and a writing coach. You'll know a lot more about me by the time this book is through, but you'll also know a lot more about yourself. This book is an invitation to consider and claim your own experiences, to question what's typical and commonly accepted, and to speak the truth. We are all Sovereign here. We are all gloriously human, and we are all channels for divine light.

In this book, you'll meet Irish goddesses, saints, and ancient queens. You'll be invited to explore a world of myth you might never have encountered before. You may decide to draw your own Sovereignty Map and start telling your own Sovereign stories thanks to the writing prompts you'll find at the close of each chapter. Many of these ideas may be new to you, so I want to give you a quick introduction to the concepts that are at the heart of this work. We'll dive deeper into all of them as we journey together, but it's important to fill your satchel of understanding with the basics before we begin.

Sovereign and Sovereignty: You are called to stand Sovereign in your own life. When you are Sovereign, you know who you are and what you want. You know how you're called to show up, heal, and serve this world. Your Sovereignty is your sacred sense of self. It is your sense of agency and your ability to exert a healthy measure of control over your thoughts, your actions, and your destiny. Your Sovereignty is your inviolable right to physical, emotional, and spiritual freedom. When you embody Sovereignty, you have full access to your creative potential, and, as you'll soon see, you'll use those gifts to make this world more equitable and more enchanting for all. Throughout this book, I'll capitalize both of these words. Your Sovereignty really is that important.

Archetypes: You'll soon meet the princess, the queen, and the wise woman, the three essential archetypes of the Sovereignty Knot. "Archetype" comes from a Greek word that means "original pattern." Certain characters appear throughout human history, teaching us about the common concerns and passions we all seem to share. The three archetypes we'll explore in this book represent particular kinds of experiences and energies present in women's lives. This unique trinity of archetypes in the Sovereignty Knot is inspired by the myths of Ireland, my own experiences, and the experiences of women I've met along the way.

Celtic Spirituality: "Celtic" means different things to different people, especially when you start talking with linguists and scholars. For the purposes of this book, Celtic spirituality refers to a modern worldview that has its ancient roots in the early Christian and pre-Christian world. My own understanding of it is rooted in a deep reverence for a Mother Goddess, the sanctity of the land, and the elements of creation: earth, air, fire, water, and spirit. Though closely associated with Ireland, Scotland,

Wales, and other regions along the western edge of Europe, you don't have to stand at the edge of the North Atlantic to experience Celtic spirituality as a way of life. Though these ideas may inspire you to dive deeper into this living theology, it's not necessary to adopt these beliefs in order to begin your journey into Sovereignty.

Irish Myth: My perspective on Sovereignty is inspired by the myth and folklore of Ireland, a country I see as my soul and my imagination's true homeland. In Ireland, the earth itself is a divine feminine force. The Sovereignty Goddess that emerges in Irish myth is at once the land beneath our feet and the otherworldly woman who appears to advocate for the sanctity of the earth and the well-being of its people. Again, you don't need to "believe" in these goddesses in order to benefit from these stories and ideas, but I have a feeling you'll fall in love with their stories.

The Sovereignty Knot: This metaphor works at multiple levels throughout this book. It is inspired by the design of a Celtic knot, those intricate and infinite patterns that have become a symbol of magic and mysticism across the world. The Sovereignty Knot has three points, representing the three main archetypes. It has no beginning and no end and represents the way we constantly cycle through the archetypes of princess, queen, and wise woman throughout our lives. It also speaks to the way many of us feel tied up in knots as we try to negotiate our various roles and navigate the endless contradictions of life.

Women: All beings on this planet have a right to Sovereignty. This work focuses on the Sovereignty of women because, even after the tremendous gains of recent history, we still live in a patriarchal system that represses women's rights and the inherent power of the feminine. "Women" is intended as an inclusive word that invites all people who identify as women to join the circle. This work is open to all who resonate with these particular archetypes of Sovereignty

The stories of Sovereignty you will read here are a glorious snare of goofing up, getting clear, being stuck, and shining bright. These are stories of rebellion and resolution, of love and loss, of traveling far to come home to yourself. You're invited to find yourself in these tales, even though it may seem that you and I may have little in common, at least at first, besides a desire for more freedom, more agency, more love, and more magic in our lives. You're invited to find your own tangle of fears and hopes, roles and responsibilities in these pages. You're invited to see the snares that culture, society, family, and your own expectations have set for you. You're invited to decide what Sovereignty is— and isn't—meant to be in your life, your work, and your love.

Again, *fáilte*. Welcome. I'm so glad you're here.

CHAPTER 1

The Straight Lines and
Spirals of Sovereignty

We women are creatures of curves and spirals, of circles and spheres. We navigate the contradictory nature of our roles and goals, dreams and fears every day. We are a beautiful, intricate design. We are a terrible tangle. We are alive with the artistry of creation and all its chaos.

Each one of us moves through the knots of Sovereignty each day. We are independent, Sovereign beings, each here on our own personal quest. And yet, we are all in this together, our fates forever bound to the fate of the collective. We constantly move between caring for the self and caring for others, balancing our own needs and desires within the great web of creation. We are Sovereign souls living one great, interconnected dream.

In this book, we'll dance together over thousands of words to find a definition for Sovereignty, and ultimately, you'll simply be guided to find your own. Sometimes, the simplest answer is the best. When my five-year-old asked me, "What's women's Sovereignty?" I responded, "It's the power to know who you are, what you want, and how you want to help people and the planet."

To be Sovereign is to stand fully in your own power. At the practical level, when you're Sovereign, you take conscious, compassionate responsibility for your own choices and your responses to the world around you. At the magical level, when you're Sovereign, you fully embody your divine-human self while your feet are rooted into a wild embrace with the earth and your hair is all spangled with stars.

When you're Sovereign, you're a clear-eyed, compassionate, confident woman with an unshakable belief in your own purpose and your own promise who is dedicated to living a life marked by peace and passion. But we cannot leave this exploration of Sovereignty there. To see this merely as an individual journey leads to a life of self-absorption and complacency that just might veer into, "Phew, I got mine! Now take me to the beach!" The goal isn't to craft a new gospel of selfishness. When you're Sovereign, you're grounded in self-love and self-worth so you can be strong and supple enough to care for your family, your community, the global community, and the earth.

Women's Sovereignty is often so closely associated with self-reliance that you might be wondering if you're being invited to walk away from everything you know and love and embrace a lone wolf sort of lifestyle. That's absolutely not required—unless you decide the next chapter of your Sovereign story needs to be about that kind of radical transformation. This is not a book about a divorce or a long solo walk across a continent. I'm in the thick of motherhood, and I'm married to a guy I met in a bar fifteen years ago. Though I occasionally dream about the life I'm not living—the one where I'm a single college professor who fills her campus apartment with cats and books and takes luxurious sabbaticals to Europe—I am fully committed to finding myself and my Sovereignty amidst the anarchy of family life.

Sovereign isn't a synonym for solitary. It's got nothing to do with isolationism. Though Sovereignty does have everything to do with independence, it has just as much to do with interdependence, too. Sovereignty is about relationships. Just remember that personal Sovereignty is an inside job and your relationship with yourself comes first. Always. Everything they say about "put on your oxygen mask first" and "you can't pour from an empty cup" is true. The Sovereign woman does not lose herself in servitude when she serves others. Neither does she seek to rule in order to amplify her own glory. She does not do this work to get drunk with power. The mark of a true Sovereign is what she does to maintain her own energy even as she pays it forward, passing on her gifts in order to empower others to set out on their own path to Sovereignty.

A Working Definition of Sovereignty that Works For Us

This book is a collection of spiraling stories, mythic goddesses, and timeless archetypes that will help us find our way to Sovereignty. These creative, imaginative concepts are potent and compelling, but we always need to ground the magical in the practical. The spirals of imagination must be anchored by straight lines of organization if you want to communicate and replicate your ideas. We need to lay down a few straight lines so we can make sense of how these visions can influence our everyday reality. The dictionary is a great place to start.

Since "sovereignty" is an old word with lots of historical baggage, it can be helpful to consider what the average *New York Times* reader might think you mean when you begin to use the word in everyday conversation. Considering this word's connection with nation states, political borders, and the wars waged to protect them, "sovereignty" might seem to rest firmly in the hands of the oppressors. In this book, we're going to look beyond newspaper headlines, cable news chyrons, and Twitter rage to find the word's ancient roots. We're going to reclaim it from the ragged jaws of history and reveal Sovereignty for what it is: a source of shared freedom, power, love, and magic.

Look up "sovereignty" and you'll find definitions like "supreme power" and "freedom from external control." Some dictionaries offer us "autonomy" while others emphasize "authority" and "rightful status, independence, or prerogative." From a certain angle, they're all relevant to our discussion, but these particular references to rights, freedom, and independence sound like they belong on a plaque commemorating the American Revolution rather than here in a woman's guide to using her voice, making an impact, feeling safe and respected in her body, and finding her share of ecstatic, connected joy along the way.

This *is* a book about revolution, but our focus is on the individual internal transformation that comes before great societal change. The details related to the rise and fall of twenty-first century regimes will linger along the outer edges of everything we talk about, but we're more focused on the first part of the "personal equals political" equation. While we're going to keep one foot firmly planted in the social reality, rife with systemic oppression and cruelty that *must* be examined and transformed, we're not doing that by wading through the minutiae of current events. Instead, we're considering the state of Sovereignty one woman at a time with the conviction that the transformed individual will shift the tides of the collective experience.

There's one dictionary definition of sovereign that's obscure, but especially important here: the idea of having the "generalized curative powers" of a sovereign remedy. Once upon a time, peddlers sold nerve tonics and other herbal potions that promised to cure all ills. Most of that stuff probably deserved the label "snake oil." Our Sovereignty remedy is different, however. This is the kind of healing elixir that really *works*. Will declaring your right to personal, creative, and spiritual self-determination cure everything and suddenly change the world? No, but it's a vital first step. When you nourish yourself in order to restore your own Sovereignty, you are preparing yourself to offer healing to the world. To affect the geopolitical landscape, or even get something to change at the village hall, you have to do your own work first. You start in your body, mind, and heart and then you move out into your yard or garden. That's where you get grounded and learn to use the energy of the earth herself to give you strength, confidence, and endurance. Then, you are able to transform the emotional ecosystem inside your home and throughout your family system. Rooted into healthy, loving relationships (perhaps after a period of uprooting and reseeding), you are able to reach into the community and across our digital web and do the work of making the world more beautiful, bearable, and bold.

Though words and the power of language are key to this work, the dictionary is our most primitive guide. We're here to call on myth, nature, and more than a little bit of magic. Rather than looking to corrupt contemporary leaders and the crimes taking place at various borders across the world to help us determine the value of Sovereignty, we're going to look to the Celtic Sovereignty Goddess as she appears in Irish and Welsh mythology and consider her cultural resonance today. This character who took shape hundreds and even thousands of years ago is actually the best equipped to help us manage the past, present, and future. I'm so excited to introduce you.

You don't need to claim Irish, Scottish, or Welsh heritage or know a thing about the Celts or the other ancient Europeans who preceded them to embrace this old-is-new story of Sovereignty. Sovereignty is a personal odyssey guided by your own gods and the places your body and spirit call home. Where your ancestors lived, where you live, and who lived on that land before you arrived all matter to your understanding of Sovereignty.

Though I spent a couple of years in Ireland in my early twenties and feel a soul-deep, ancestral connection to that part of the world, I'm an American woman of mixed European heritage who grew up with all of the privileges of being white, straight, and middle class. I grew up on land originally inhabited by the Wampanoag people on what is now called Cape Cod, Massachusetts. Now, I live in a region referred to as the Hudson Valley of New York on land that was once inhabited by the Lenape people. I acknowledge that the white settlers who came hundreds of years before me violated the Sovereignty of those tribes, taking the land through outrageous bargains or outright theft. I acknowledge that I benefit from those invasions and that colonization is an ongoing process. If you are a non-native person living in the United States, Canada, New Zealand, or Australia, I invite you to research the peoples who lived on the land before you and consider the practice of Land Acknowledgement, which is becoming more common in colonized territories across the world.[1]

Ultimately, your Sovereignty needs to be grounded in your experiences, your identity, and the soil beneath your feet. And yet, contemporary personal Sovereignty is enacted in relationship with history, religion, and culture—and much of it is ugly, divisive, and painful. Let's recognize that. Let's watch that. Let's celebrate our commonalities, acknowledge our differences, make reparations, and be mindful that the past inflects the present. Let's commit to the belief that we all can transform the future together.

Develop Your Own Sovereign "Why"

We'll begin with three reasons to embody the most Sovereign version of yourself. Later in this book, you'll be prompted to develop your own answer to the question, "Why Sovereignty?"

You're invited to stand in your Sovereignty so you can

- fully inhabit your power, your magic, and your self-worth
- transform your relationship to age and time
- use your own growing power to empower others

When you're certain of your power and your value, when you believe in your own magic, and when you are able to navigate

---

1 For more on the purpose and practice of Land Acknowledgement, visit the U.S. Department of Arts and Culture at https://usdac.us/nativeland/ and download their free guide.

aging and time on your own terms, you are Sovereign. You can do anything, whether that's forging a new relationship with your body, heading a company, leaving a dead-end partnership, transforming how you parent your children, (re)kindling a truly nurturing love affair, or stepping up to organize for social change.

Let's take a closer look at "the why of Sovereignty." Everything we explore together, no matter what archetype we're talking about—and we will get to the princess, the queen, and the wise woman shortly—will come back to these essential themes.

In a way, **self-worth** is easy to understand conceptually, but, at least in my experience, it's something that's hard to maintain. Years ago, I interviewed several entrepreneurial and community-minded women for a local magazine. One wise woman spoke of the importance of having "an unshakable sense of self-regard." I remember being entranced and mystified by this Jedi mind trick. Considering that we live in a consumerist regime that profits from our self-doubt, liking yourself is a rebellious act. Back then, I wondered how old I'd have to be and what I'd have to accomplish in order to inhabit such a space. Now I know it's not about time or experience, but is instead about consciously cultivating self-love, self-trust, and a deep commitment to your own worthiness. When I could consistently stand in this truth, I was ready not to just dream about Sovereignty, but to be it and teach it.

And sometimes believing in yourself after years of self-doubt can feel like **magic.** When I talk about magic I'm not talking about card tricks, rabbits, and top hats. Though I love to call myself a Word Witch, I'm not necessarily talking about the deliberate spellwork that modern-day witches and shamans practice. I've adopted the definition of magic made popular by Starhawk, the ecofeminist and leading voice in the Neopaganism movement: "Magic is the art of changing consciousness at will."[2] This seems to keep all options open in a way that I rather like. It makes this magic business intensely practical, too. To believe in your own magic is to believe in your own creativity, connectedness, and potential.

Power might be harder to wrap your head and heart around. Sovereignty is not about being better than anyone else or about using power over others. This work is meant to be a feminine/feminist redefinition that decouples power from the old patterns of domination and control. Think of power as life force that you can choose to channel in service to the highest personal and collective good. You may wield your power with a lullaby or with a warrior cry.

Then there's "**Women's Time**," a term coined by French feminist psychoanalytic philosopher Julia Kristeva in an essay of the same name.[3] She believed we needed an alternative to the linear understanding of time that simply tracked wars, invasions, and the other trappings of "history" with its blatant emphasis on the *his*. Women's Time is an invitation to measure life according to cyclical, natural time of the body—particularly the kinds of bodies that make babies. It gives you a holistic understanding of how you are a reflection of nature and how you are in relationship with nature, especially the moon and the seasons. This understanding of Women's Time opens us up to what I call

---

2 Starhawk, *Truth or Dare: Encounters with Power, Authority, and Mystery* (San Francisco: Harper Collins, 1987), 6. Starhawk attributes the quote to early twentieth-century occultist and novelist Dion Fortune but does not provide an original source.

3 Julia Kristeva, *The Kristeva Reader,* edited by Toril Moi (New York: Columbia University Press, 1986), 187–213.

Sovereign Time. When we challenge the linear understanding of time, we also challenge what we think we know about aging and what each decade of life is "supposed" to look like.

There's a commonly accepted framework of the feminine life cycle that breaks a woman's experience into the phases of maiden, mother, and crone. Many women have grown up loving this concept, but Sovereign Time asks you to tear it apart. In a culture obsessed with the hero's journey and the cult of youth, it's rare and wonderful to see the valorization of the mother or to see the elder feminine represented at all, but we deserve more. To define a woman by virginity, motherhood, and menopause is too bloody limiting for complex creatures like us. This model assumes that womanhood is defined by biology, which it is not, and it also traps us in static, time-bound roles. What is generally passed off as ancient goddess wisdom was actually codified in 1948 by a man named Robert Graves in a book called *The White Goddess*. This interpretation of the triple goddess attempts to celebrate women at all phases of life, but it's tragically linear. When you leave the "sweet young thing" label behind and move up to become a queen, it's like receiving a promotion. Unfortunately, we almost never celebrate the movement into cronehood in the same way. Though we tend to love our grannies, the elderly woman is either rendered invisible or is quietly despised. The hag is dressed in the patriarchy's fear and loathing, and that influences everyone's perspective, even the most ardent feminists amongst us.

As I hit forty, fully immersed in motherhood and realizing I'm nearer to the crone than I am to the maiden (at least chronologically), I really started to see the limitations of this framework. We're not accessing the fullness of our magic and our potential when we're trapped in the inexorable progression of history. I want to give us all permission to dissolve our obsessive devotion to uncomplicated beginning-middle-end thinking and embrace what the mystics and the quantum theorists have long been trying to tell us: Time doesn't relentlessly move along the straight line to which we've all been taught to conform. Reality is much more multifaceted and multilayered. This is why I took my knowledge of myth, my love of fairytales, my feminist politics, my own lived experiences, and my observations of the women around me and in our culture and devised my own trinity of archetypes: the princess, the queen, and the wise woman.

I see these three distinct archetypes in every woman (and in people who identify as women and in any human willing to transcend the bullshit gender roles that tell us only chicks can understand and identify with feminine symbols). We constantly cycle through these archetypes throughout our lives. As you'll see when you meet the princess, queen, and wise woman below, we need access to all of their various qualities to lead healthy lives and achieve a state of wholeness. No single archetype can stand alone. It's only when you integrate the three that you truly embody your Sovereignty.

Meet the Archetypes of the Sovereignty Knot: Princess, Queen, and Wise Woman

At the outset, I mentioned that, as individuals, we are both a beautiful, intricate design as well as a terrible tangle. In fact, we *are* the Sovereignty Knot. We get tied up in the knots of Sovereignty as we try to maintain our sense of personal agency within the structures of family and society, but the Sovereignty Knot is more than just a difficult puzzle to solve. The Sovereignty

Knot is also a symbol of profound unity that represents the relationship between three essential archetypes in a woman's life.

A Celtic knot represents an endless continuum. Think of one of those ancient illuminated manuscripts from the Irish monasteries or the screen-printed designs you see on the tapestries at the local hippy shop. Having no beginning and no end, a Celtic knot shows us that we are part of an infinity cycle, swooping upward, doubling back, circling round, diving down until the next turning point takes us through the figure once again, and on forever. Now, imagine the three-pointed symbol called a trinity knot or a triquetra. This is the Sovereignty Knot that represents the archetypes of princess, queen, and wise woman.

Free the Princess.
Crown the Queen.
Embrace the Wise Woman.

If there's any sort of Sovereignty formula, this is it. "Free the princess. Crown the queen. Embrace the wise woman" came in like a download some years ago. Over time, I've refined the way I word it. Over a lifetime, I'll refine the way I live it.

You are the heroine of your own Sovereignty story, just as I'm the heroine of mine. We all have our own version of the Sovereignty archetypes within us, and they'll manifest in their own unique way as we adventure through life. That said, we are more alike than we are different. The universal energies of the princess, the queen, and the wise woman vibrate inside all of us and help us access our Sovereignty.

> *Sovereignty depends on freeing the princess*
> *(your sexy, brave, carefree parts).*
>
> *Sovereignty depends on crowning the queen*
> *(your capable, responsible, compassionate parts).*
>
> *Sovereignty depends on embracing the wise woman*
> *(your still, irreverent, insightful parts).*

The archetypes of princess, queen, and wise woman are here to teach us to uncover, interrogate, and celebrate all aspects of our Sovereignty. I want this kind of insight for you, for my daughters, and for myself. I want it for my husband, my dad, and the people in Congress, too, by the way. We'll fold in the men in our lives and the larger structures of society as we go—we're always called to enact this Sovereignty quest against the backdrop of domestic and collective life—but this work happens one awakening at a time.

As with the archetypes themselves, the specific qualities assigned to the princess, queen, and wise woman are a product of my eclectic study of mythology and human psychology. Many of these ideas are informed by conversations with my writing coaching and story healing clients. People come to me when they need help accessing their personal, creative, and spiritual Sovereignty and when they want to turn these revelations into stories they can share with the world. I'm blessed to learn from such brave and vulnerable storytellers who use writing as part of their healing and awakening. And now, I'm excited to develop these ideas in *The Sovereignty Knot*, drawing together all I've learned through a blend of practical magic, great books, wise mentors, tarot spreads, hard work, a deep stretch, a good cry, a long walk, a longer talk, a lingering kiss, and well-honed intuition.

Let's begin with a basic sketch of each archetype including her powers and unhealthy patterns, her knots and contradictions, how she is often perceived in the world, where she roams, and what she carries with her along the way.

Meet the Princess

> *Her powers:* freedom, potential, experimentation, vitality, physicality, boldness, innocence, sexuality, awakening, imagination, play, adventure, optimism

> *Her unhealthy patterns:* messy mistakes, irresponsibility, low self-esteem, lack of self-worth, unhealthy risk-

taking, chronic neediness, promiscuity, bingeing, addiction, self-centeredness, victimhood, fear of the unknown, escapism

Her knots and contradictions: She is the flow of dependence and independence, proudly walking alone and desperately needing to hold someone's hand. She is free from the constraints of relationship and yet she lavishes great energy on finding, pleasing, and keeping a mate or a group of companions.

How the outside world tends to perceive her: Full of possibility and promise, yet too young and too foolish. Sexy and desirable, and yet too pure and too inexperienced. The center of attention, and yet also too naive and too irresponsible.

Her territory: She is the one who dwells on the cliff, throwing wild parties out there one night and spending the next feeling terribly alone. She lives between the worlds: part civilization and part wilderness. She walks the edge between the known world and the great expanse beyond.

Her tools: Boots. Actually, she has two pairs. She's well served by sturdy hiking boots that hold up in all weather as she explores new terrain. The other pair is made of buttery leather and has the perfect heel. She's almost always willing to risk the twisted ankles for the sake of fashion and the power she feels when she's stalking through the night.

Meet the Queen

Her powers: creation, birth, manifestation, leadership, commitment, responsibility, structure, righteous rage, passionate change, protection, nurturing, stability, balance

Her unhealthy patterns: controlling, self-sacrificing, scarcity-driven, power-hungry, defensive, judgmental, self-absorbed, manipulative

Her knots and contradictions: She is tied down by relationships with partner, children, and other dependents and she is joyfully enmeshed with these people who matter most. She is the rock, both the calm loving center and the weighty ballast that everyone depends on and takes for granted. She is the ultimate benevolent ruler, and yet she can use her power to coerce and dominate.

How the outside world tends to perceive her: A capable, remarkable leader, yet also a domineering ballbuster. A maternal force of nature, yet also a frumpy, past-her-prime killjoy. A deeply devoted caregiver, yet also a person without boundaries.

Her territory: The castle where she welcomes family, community, and the stranger. She may look the world over for the perfect palace, but ultimately it's about creating her own home that is safe, comfortable, and open to those who need her shelter, guidance, and love.

Her tools: The cup. Two cups, actually. One she offers to others, taking the role as the conveyor of power and Sovereignty. The other cup is hers, and she drinks deep and fills it regularly with her own magic, her own elixir, her own particularly audacious and intoxicating passions.

Meet the Wise Woman

Her powers: spirituality, equanimity, acceptance, stillness, divine surrender, insight, humor, irreverence, renewal, alchemy, completion, wholeness

Her unhealthy patterns: depression, isolation, passivity, stagnation, spiritual bypassing, fear of change

Her knots and contradictions: She makes what she wants and barely cares if things don't turn out well. She is all complete unto herself, but sometimes yearns for the brilliant passion and cozy chaos of her past. She is fully in relationship with herself and with the divine and still tries to maintain her human connections, too. At peace with her sexuality, she either consciously closes that chapter or finds a way to fold it into her present. She's likely to make a bawdy joke and see the erotic in the midst of feigned innocence.

How the outside world tends to perceive her: The venerated elder, but also the creature who moves too slowly and needs too much. The keeper of cultural and ancestral knowledge, yet also the voice of outgrown traditions and a reminder of a past no one wants to bother with. The source of sweet nostalgia, but also a reminder of a difficult history and the truth of "the bad old days."

Her territory: The cave that is both the birth canal and the tomb. She hides away in there both to be free from the madness of the world and to pray for the salvation of the world. Considered to be a recluse, she is open to those who are willing to test themselves in finding her.

Her tools: Silence and conversation. She relishes both the wordlessness of nature and a good chat by the fire. Unconcerned with the material world, the wise woman is more interested in the company she keeps. Sometimes, she just wants to hold court with the wind, but other times she's keen on an intimate conversation that gets to the heart of creation.

The Lived Reality of Sovereignty

Do you see bits of yourself in all of these, regardless of your age and experiences? Good. I do, too. We're meant to inhabit all of these identities throughout life—both the lovely parts and the shameful parts, too. You're invited to celebrate the princess, the queen, and the wise woman, forgive them of their trespasses, and ask them about their needs and their pain. You're invited to recognize that you've always been all three archetypes all along. You're entering the Sovereignty Knot because you're ready to recognize that you have access to any and all of their energies at every stage of life.

Let's do a quick reality check before we start exploring the stories, both ancient and modern, that are designed to help you deepen your understanding of Sovereignty. Spirals of theory and make-believe won't get us very far in a daily reality plagued with violence, bigotry, and environmental degradation. Though these archetypes are associated with characters that seem to come from a storybook, we're on a mission to make the magic they represent into a very real force in our lives.

I have been rubbing elbows with the Sovereignty Goddess since I was a college student fascinated by Irish literature and Celtic culture. Once I left academia, I sort of forgot about all the old stories that had once kindled my imagination and spoke to my soul. More than a decade later, everything came rushing back to me when my spiritual teacher Eleanora Amendolara declared, "The goal is to stand Sovereign in your own reality." That single sentence from my mentor was responsible for launching the Irish goddess right back into my everyday consciousness. Suddenly, Sovereignty was no longer just an intriguing concept from my past. Sovereignty reemerged in full color and reminded me it was always supposed to be at the core of my life and work. Everything I'd been seeking through the first years of adulthood was right there: the desire for agency and self-reliance, a sense of belonging to this earth, and an abiding love for myself and my world. In Sovereignty, I could find the medicine that would integrate that wide open young woman I was with the mother I am today and the glorious hag I hope one day to be. It would help me consciously bend time so I could integrate the powers and energies of each phase into my life, regardless of age or experience.

It's important to acknowledge the inherent peril that comes with this idea of standing Sovereign in your own reality. It brings us dangerously close to that bad old New Age cop out, "you create your own reality." The approach I'm advocating for is the opposite of spiritual bypassing that declares that your problems result from a lack of positive thinking. When you're Sovereign, you don't expect hopes and prayers to change everything—at least not until they are accompanied by inspired conscious action. That said, keep praying. Keep talking with friends and advisors about what to do to improve the political and planetary climate and how to manage the uncertainty that's part of everyday life. We are all in this together. Our kind of self-reliance isn't about suffering alone, even when—especially when—you're struggling personally and the institutions you may have been taught to believe in seem to be going through a collective dark night of the soul. It's my hope that you have a community of like-minded, like-hearted people to surround you, but remember you also have the archetypes of Sovereignty to guide you. Archetypes are a reflection of the soul of the world, and that soul has always been vast enough to hold every shade of dark and light and still remain strong and whole.

I'll Tell You My Sovereign Stories So You Can Tell Yours

This book and my entire approach to Sovereignty are a response to the misguided belief that any one lifetime is to be lived in a straightforward, logical way that's described in the scriptures, the etiquette guides, or the success manuals. Let's challenge the lies that tell us that following the rules, playing it cool, and sticking to someone else's strategy will make you the winner. Screw the scoring system that's based on position, prestige, party loyalty, money in the bank, and dying with the most toys. We are part of an immense, interconnected system that encompasses everything from cells to stars. All of us are always part of the spiral, the energy that moves from the edges to the center, round and round like the sun and the moon and the seasons. We are here to go with the flow, and we recognize the improvisational energy that courses through the patterns of nature itself. There is room to zig and zag, to color outside the lines, to screw it up royally, and then to come back to the core, to your Sovereign sense of self, in order to feel renewed.

We're here to bust the limitations of linear chronology, but it's true that we spend certain phases of life employing one archetype's power more than others. Right now, you'd look at me and see me queen-ing my tail off every day. It's my blessing (and yes, sometimes it's my burden) to be raising a pair of young maidens right now. Thing is, even as I work to embody the role of mama and need to draw on all my power to lead, nurture, and hold steady in order to create a safe space for my girls to grow, I cannot escape my princess self in the process. She's not ready to let me go, either. I want to—I need to—hold onto my wide-eyed innocence so I can be the unencumbered virgin as well as the lust-fueled lass. She's the one who will teach me to respect the intensity and the recklessness I see in my own daughters. She's the one who will remind me that my own wild abandon on the playground—and lusty orgasms in the bedroom—are meant to be enjoyed today and every day of my long and luscious life. The princess helps me see how to be a better mom, and she also helps me remember that I'm more than "just" a mom.

And, by the same token, I need to channel my own inner wise woman in this stage of life—especially since my grandmothers have long since died and I've spent most of my own decade of motherhood without a mother of my own to guide me. When I hear my voice rise and my anger shift out of constructive righteous rage aimed at challenging hegemonic systems of power and into the unchecked madness of a woman who has lost her center, I remember I have the option to come home to the wiser aspect of myself. I can rest and heal at her hearth fire until I am ready to face the world with equanimity and some measure of control. The wise woman is someone I am growing toward, certainly, but, more than that, she is the symbol of my original stillness, the great expanse that comes before and after this explosive evolutionary process of being alive.

Sovereignty appeared out of the mists of western Ireland for me, but she dwells in every corner of the globe and exists everywhere on the corners of your own life's map. Sovereignty isn't a particular destination. It's a perpetual journey that follows the twists and falls and rises of an infinity knot. I hope I retain the adventurous, sensual aspects of my princess self until I die. I know that I came into this life with shades of the wise woman because, just like everyone else, I am an immortal spirit having a temporary physical experience that will be as glorious and amazing as I can make it. I have the power and potential to step in and become queen of my own life, right now in this midlife moment, but this ability to reign was also available at six and sixteen, and it will be there for me at eighty-six and one hundred six. All of these elements of the Sovereign self are accessible at any time.

My wish for you, for me, for all people is this: Become so sure and grounded in your individual story that you cannot help but want to share your insights, compassion, and power with the collective. Become so strong in who you are that you feel prepared to reach out to hold and help with one arm and hold back the tide of distraction, disaffection, and cruelty with the other. Become Sovereign in your own life, in your own spirit, in your own creativity so you can stand for everyone else's right to be Sovereign in theirs.

There won't be many straight lines in this book, so let's begin with one of the curviest spots in the world: an Irish country road.

Writing Prompt: Your Map of Sovereignty

Each chapter of this book will include at least one writing prompt. As a writing coach and the founder of the Sovereign Writers Circle, I know that writing prompts are the best way to help you access your inner wisdom and see your thoughts, emotions, and dreams in a new way. But sometimes we need to play and doodle before we're ready to start constructing our ideas into sentences.

Take out a piece of paper and sketch out a map like you might see at the start of an epic novel. This is a map of your own Sovereign territory. This is a map of courage and desire, of promises broken and trust restored. This map shows you where you've been in the past and where you are right now. It has the power to hold your future and all that you imagine you might see someday. It's also a map of myth and story, both your own lived legends and the ancient lore that holds us all. There's no right or wrong here. There is only freedom and possibility.

You decide the size and shape, whether it's an island or whether it's bordered by friendly realms and difficult

---

neighbors. You may be inspired by the descriptions of the territory of each archetype and start to fill in certain geographical features and place-names right now.

My own Sovereignty Map includes places like A Cave of Initiation, A Garden for Weeping, and A Cliff for Stargazing and Drinking Songs. Your map might include A Meadow for Lovers and A Hill to Climb Alone. You can populate this map with memories from your own life or simply use this as a space to dream.

As you proceed through this book, come back to your map. Add to it, erase some borders and redraw stronger boundaries. You may find that large stretches of your terrain have been colonized by the armies of systemic oppression like sexism, racism, homophobia, and transphobia. It's just as likely that unfit lovers, controlling bosses, and children who haven't yet learned to blaze their own way have taken up unlawful residence on your land. And by that, I mean your body, your mind, your heart, and your soul. As you come to know this territory and begin to understand your own power, your own worth, and your own specific style of Sovereignty, you'll gather the tools you need to draft eviction notices and reclaim who you really are. You'll discover new places and rediscover forgotten wonders that have been part of your Sovereign territory all along.

Remember that even the most comprehensive map in the world can't keep you from getting lost. It's inevitable in a world this big and this wild. And, of course, it's in the getting lost that you find yourself.

CHAPTER 2

Entering the Cave

It was an indifferent sort of Irish morning, a bit of gray sweater weather that didn't necessarily promise sunshine or rain. It was enough for us. We were tourists with a warm, dry car who'd just had a full breakfast, complete with black pudding, fried up for us in a big house in County Mayo. The hospitality was a blessing to be sure, but we needed to be in Roscommon by noon. I wanted to get out of this twenty-first century castle and into the wilds. Someone was waiting for us, and he promised to show us a place that was at once the birthplace of the goddess and the gateway to hell.

When my aunt, my twenty-something cousin, and my eight-year-old daughter finally got into the car, I was tight lipped and silent. Every part of me was on the move—except my actual body that had to sit in the driver's seat as everyone wedged their American luggage into a European car. With about four days of experience driving on the left side of narrow roads, I was finally ready to drive the speed limit—and exceed it. But with all the twists and turns and crowded main streets that stretched between us and the village of Tulsk, I realized that no amount of white-knuckle speeding (and "Oh, Jesus, Marisa, that was close!" comments) could get us there on time.

There was nothing to do but practice some magic.

I'd tried this before when I was back home in the Hudson Valley. Then, I'd wanted to save my daughter from that dreaded feeling of being the last one left at the curb. Do you remember the waves of rage and fear of abandonment that used to wash over you before you had a concept of traffic or understood that your mother had more to do than wait for you to be done with school? Those kid fears still burn in me, and I'd do a lot to save my girls from such experiences, but my worries about their righteous indignation was nothing compared to what I was feeling here on the N60 road. We were speeding to the place I was most eager and most afraid to explore, and I couldn't stand to miss it just because my family needed to graze a table heavy with bacon and eggs and have just one more cup of tea.

And so, I started working on the underside of time.

My hands were on the steering wheel, but my fingers were actually wrapped around the knots of energy that lay beneath the surface of the earth. I was trying to find the strands of time and space that are layered beneath our understanding of the moment. I was tugging at the fabric of the universe, and though I had no idea what I was doing, somehow I understood exactly how it had to be done. Clearly, I was messing with something bigger than me, something that would have consequences. Though I've long been someone who likes to talk about magic, I have rarely gathered the courage or the focus to risk the *doing* of it. That's the tricky thing about believing in magic—you're also wise enough to be a little bit afraid of it, or at least in awe of it. If "magic is the art of changing consciousness at will," I need to admit that I'm both excited and terrified of change and the mystery of consciousness. But then, Sovereignty relies on recognizing your own power to shift your experience by shifting your perceptions. The real trick of magic (and Sovereignty) is simply in believing you know how and then giving it a try.

Was I actually altering the space-time continuum as we sped to County Roscommon? Was there any risk of changing the distant future or somehow shortening my own life as I attempted to stretch and fold time on this particular April morning? Or was I just soothing my own frustrations with fantasies that I could use the power of my intentions to slow the clock or move the ponderous truck to the shoulder of the road?

All I know is that it worked.

Because I focused less on worry and more on magic, my family was spared the nasty sounding "hurry *up*" that welled in my throat. Added bonus: I felt like a sorceress (and proved myself to be a badass "wrong side of the road" driver). Most importantly, we ended up beating our guide to the meeting point and we were set for a day that would change my consciousness in powerful, lasting ways.

If you want to credit our peaceful, timely arrival to my self-control, luck, and coincidence, be my guest, but honestly, I think you get more out of calling it magic. This "what you see is what you get" perspective on the world never explains all the miracles, synchronicities, and sacred experiences we witness every blessed day. Stubborn pragmatism labels these moments of wonder and connection as mere whimsy, delusion, or child's play, but that approach robs us of the best parts of being alive. Sovereignty is about rooting into real life and transforming suffering, division, and oppression. Sovereignty, as I choose to define and embody it, is also about conspiring with your imagination to reach spiritual depths and mysteries unseen.

As you come to believe in your own inherent power and get to know the archetypes that dwell within, you'll realize that talking to goddesses and focusing energy on changing your own consciousness in order to change the world is more potent than sheer practicality and planning alone ever could be. The magic that lets us manipulate time and space might not quite look like stepping through the standing stones and entering another century like they do in *Outlander*, but it looks everything like the life I crave. Real life is full of real magic and it's available to all of us who dare to look for it, treasure it, and conjure it.

Leaving Home to Return Home

Nearly fifteen years of "real life" stretched between me and the last time I had been in Ireland. This was the place where my inner princess roamed most freely, and here I was again, finally back, feeling more like the queen of my own life than I ever had before. I was never supposed to be away from this place for so long. My first visit was a long weekend trip to Dublin when I was a freshman in college visiting an American boy during his semester abroad. Getting my passport and booking a flight on Aer Lingus and *then* telling my parents my plans was my first radical act of independence. Soon after, I'd realize a dream that was long in the making when I spent my own junior year in Galway. After that came graduate school. That strange year was supposed to start with a flight out of Logan Airport on September 11, 2001. Eventually planes flew again and the world would rearrange itself according to new threats and fears and I would make it to Dublin, but that city would never feel like a place I could call my own. I returned one last time in 2003, limping through a trip to recapture the past with another American boyfriend who wouldn't stay in my life for long. I had no idea that I wouldn't come back until I was a mom with an eight-year-old in tow.

But here I was, defying all the stories of "not me" and "not yet" that had been piling up in my dungeon of self-limitation for over a decade. I'd half-believed the lie that I was a one-dimensional character, a dutifully married mother of two who didn't have the funds or the support to just take off to Europe to relive her princess days. Such trips were for the lucky ones, I'd have told you. Women who had mastered entrepreneurship. Wives of men with deep pockets. Chicks with partners who craved adventure and spontaneity. This kind of frivolity was for the people with mothers who would love to stay with the the grandkids for a week. I'd survived too much and risked too little to deserve this trip—or so I had told myself throughout my thirties as one year melted into the next and the closest thing I had to comfort was "someday." Someday I'll get back there. Someday I'll have the money and the freedom. Someday I will find myself back where I belong.

I wouldn't just wake up in Ireland, of course. It would take planning and action on my part. Before any of that, it would take a conscious awakening to my own worthiness and to the "yes" within me. Sovereignty may be an internal phenomenon, but the universe conspires to get us to agree to our own power. After my aunt suggested we take the trip, I pulled two cards from a goddess-inspired tarot deck. One was the goddess Brigid and the other—you can't make this stuff up—depicted a pot of gold at the end of the rainbow. And then, everything changed. Suddenly, simply purchasing the plane tickets meant I was practicing magic. Every action after that seemed blessed and inevitable. Rush passports for my daughter and me. Strategizing about how my husband would solo parent our four-year-old with help from my dad. Reconnecting with the college friends who would host us during our visit. Finding the right balance between making plans and leaving things to chance. Each little choice was a line in this new Sovereignty story that wove together my meandering princess past, the emerging confidence of my queen, and the power of the place that sourced all of my wise woman energy.

It was the final day of our ten-day trip. Galway had been our home base and that gave us the chance to visit my favorite places on earth: the rocky expanses of the Burren in County Clare and the largest of the Aran Islands, Inis Mór. We'd explored Achill Island and visited the castle of a pirate queen and a few other places that were new to me in County Mayo, but it was only on the last day I would explore totally unknown territory, the ancient site of Rathcroghan.

Perhaps it would help the story to declare that I had known about Rathcroghan and its mythic cave called Oweynagat for decades.

Wouldn't it be romantic to say I'd been longing to visit this place ever since I'd heard its legends from my grandmother or from the old innkeeper who offered me milky tea and biscuits during my first visit to Ireland? Some of the most meaningful stories get a chance to work on us for years, to fill us with a sort of friendly longing as we grow accustomed to the ache to know a place firsthand. Those are the dreams that steep long and get rooted deep. Sometimes, those are also the dreams that are the easiest to bring to the grave—all full of unrequited "someday" energy. In this case, the dream was fresh and green. I'd only read about it a year or two before when Sharon Blackie described entering the cave in her fabulous book of Celtic spirituality and ecofeminism, *If Women Rose Rooted.* Caught in my "if only" mindset, I had tried to forget about the place as soon as I read about it, but part of my imagination slipped into the rocky cleft with the writer and never came out. When I happened upon a podcast interview with a local guide who described taking people into the mysterious Oweynagat while I was planning our itinerary, I knew this was the entire reason I needed to get back to Ireland. I needed to face all my fears of narrow spaces, descend into the depths, and experience this rebirth.

Rathcroghan was once the royal seat of Medb (anglicized to "Maeve"), Ireland's most storied warrior queen. She was both woman and goddess, all Sovereignty and sexuality, all power and poise. Her sensual, sassy magic is at the heart of the greatest story in Irish myth, the *Táin Bo Cuailnge*, the story of a cattle raid gone mad. The irony isn't lost on me. I was teaching myself how to do road-trip magic so I could be there in time to meet the ghost of the wild heroine who led Ireland's most famous cross-country ride. I'll tell you more of her story later when we explore the archetype of the queen. For now, simply picture acres of green fields occasionally interrupted by stone walls and great grassy mounds. These human-made hillocks are what remains of royal settlements inhabited for thousands of years. Our guide would share historical data and bits of local lore and pepper it all with the jokes appropriate to a place where intercourse with a horse may or may not have been part of a king's coronation. But most of that was lost on me... We were too close to the cave for me to absorb the stories or the way this ancient site aligned with sacred mountains and energetic ley lines that spanned the west of Ireland.

The moment I saw our guide in his tweed jacket and shiny leather boots, I realized one of two things had to be true: The mud of Oweynagat had been oversold or this guy wasn't going to hold the flashlight for us when we stepped below the ground. The latter was true. He hadn't been in the cave for some time and he had no plans to do so that day. This is when the sensible mother, the American mother, might have had second thoughts about bringing a third grader into a rough, pitch-black hole in the ground. At least the wolves were long extinct, the snakes had never existed, and I had never heard of any poisonous insects in all my time in Ireland. It didn't occur to me to worry about whether my daughter would prove to be afraid of the dark.

As we prepared to climb in, one headlamp and two cell phone lights among the three of us, our guide pulled hawthorn buds off the bush. He told us they were good for the heart and invited us each to eat one. Suddenly, my mother was there. The mother who should have been on the trip with us, who should have made it possible for me to return years before because she would have loved to be grandmother in charge for a week as I returned to my own fountain of youth. Mammy wasn't there because she had died of a sudden, unexpected heart attack nearly eight years prior. She wasn't there, and yet she was *there*... That's been the story ever since we lost the woman who'd always created the gravitational pull that held us together. And so, hearts protected, we were ready to brave the belly of the earth.

The mouth of Oweynagat is little more than a fissure in the ground that some ancient stoneworkers made a bit bigger. When you approach, you see a low slung "v" hiding in plain sight under that protective mama, the hawthorn bush. My daughter ran right by it, clearly expecting some sort of grand entrance into a hillside. Instead, this birthing place of the goddess was as lowly as any manger. And every bit as mysterious and glorious. It was time to climb into Mother Ireland's vagina with a couple of princesses in tow. Does that sound pejorative, like I am telling you that my cousin and my daughter were worried they would muddy their hems and crush their lace and tousle their hair down in the cave? Quickly, we need to have a conversation about princesses and who they really are.

Yes, they are young (but not always young). Yes, they are concerned with beauty (but sometimes they actively court ugliness and they are not always all that beautiful, especially on the inside). Yes, they still need to be taken care of (but not always in the way you think, and certainly not in the way they think). Yes, they are headstrong and want their own way (but this is rarely about ordering others about, instead it is about a longing to live their own brave visions of what it means to be alive and be themselves).

Princesses wear heels, sure, but princesses also wear boots that will get covered in the muck and glory of the Sovereignty quest. When they are young—you can decide what "young" means to you—they're not considering the responsibility of the queen or the vision of the wise woman. Their Sovereignty is about exploration, experimentation, and the freedom to make mistakes that help them discover how they'll fit into this world. The journey into princesshood is a long one and it loops out and in, weaving to the edges of culture and then back to the center, just like the path of a Celtic knot.

My own princess self was the one who suggested this particular adventure. Who *needed* this adventure. As we entered this cave, however, I had to hold us all with the energy of the queen. I was the mother caring for her daughter and a young woman I'd always think of as my "little cousin." It was my job to make this descent into the unknown just safe enough. Queens are a bit preoccupied with safety and security, of course. We need to practice a measure of caution at every stage of life, but we look to the queen to stand at the head of the party and think of all the potential calamities before leading anyone into the dark.

The queen wears whatever costume is suitable to the occasion. There's time for the lace thong and the plunging neckline (if such fashion pleases you), or for the white suit and pumps, but it's often appropriate to rule in leggings and a T-shirt that announces your politics or your favorite band. Though she's the archetype you call on when you need to take charge, the queen doesn't need to put on her bossy pants to rule. She is there to offer care and protection, and the healthiest queens do a fine job of balancing caring for others with their own self-care and nurturance.

Since we're doing brief introductions of the princess and the queen, it's only right that you should meet the wise woman, too. Sometimes, the woman is so wise she leaves the youngsters with their fearlessness and resilient knees to explore the darkness and try their luck with the slippery stones. Though she might have a great deal in common with the crone, the wise woman isn't necessarily old. Instead, she is a being who is complete unto herself. She's much like the princess in that way, but instead of being the virgin on her own adventure or the young lover lusting after a mate, the wise woman is content to hold and contemplate the story rather than act it out. The wise woman seeks out solitude, but she's never alone for long. The princesses and queens, as well as the wisest of the wise women who know that they need the support of their sisters, will knock on her door. They come seeking tea and counsel, a place to shed tears and have a good laugh. The wise woman, of course, wears whatever she damn pleases. And if the outfit seems inappropriate for the occasion, it would probably be a good idea if the occasion shifted to meet the lady's needs and desires.

I was called to enter this cave to meet the Wise Woman in the capital letter sense. Not just the wise woman within me, but the wise woman within the world, within us all. She lives in caves, you see. She is the one who holds us tight in the dimension before this one, in the realm before birth. She is the one who welcomes us home at the other side of this human lifetime, in the realm beyond death. The wise woman is the keeper of your original self, the purest version of you that is untarnished by the expectations and masquerades of contemporary life.

But let's get back to the mud and the stones and the moment at hand. Yes, it was time to make a spiritual pilgrimage, but I had to be practical mother hen, too. If nearly a decade of motherhood has taught me anything, it's that the queen doesn't have the luxury of being precious about the transcendent. There's almost never enough time and the sacred almost always gets mixed up with the profane. The magical is going to involve mucky boots, and the mystical is going to happen in between warning a kid to watch her step and to hold hands. Maybe I was just too busy to worry about anything else, or maybe I was already wrapped in a spell of protection, but none of my typical fears got in the way: a twisted ankle or worry that the walls might start closing in. I was as invincible as a princess, as conscious as a queen, and as trusting as a wise woman who knows that Mother Earth was there to catch me with every footstep. I wasn't necessarily thinking of the Sovereignty Knot archetypes at this moment, though. By entering this cave I was simply coming into a new, true relationship with myself, with the Great Mother, and with the entirety of the earth. I was shedding my obsession with the world of the light and seeing that this was the true birthplace of my spirit and my feminine nature. And I was doing it while being somebody's mom.

Will you pause a moment with me and savor "the true birthplace of my spirit and my feminine nature"? These are words that are easy to type. I've read them before in other places with only the smallest variation, but did I ever really understand them? In truth, I think I did, but I didn't *know* I did until I emerged from the cave. This rebirthing was all so subtle and would only be perceptible to others with time, but internally, there was a quake and a shift as all the furniture in my soul was rearranged. Maybe it was more like a previously unknown section of my Sovereignty Map was unfolded and revealed. That is the way it is with the divine feminine. She may show her power in the unleashing of a storm or in the release of a passionate sigh, but you watch her come on so slowly, like the darkness after one of those endless midsummer Irish sunsets. I remember my midwives saying that "nothing ever happens quickly in a birth." They were assuring us that having a baby at home was safe because there was time to get help if we needed the resources of a hospital. Well, it seems that nothing ever happens quickly in a cave, either.

We didn't spend more than ten minutes in there, or so I'd guess. The place was beyond timeless. It took a while to negotiate the wet clay and to coach one another to find the stones that would save you from the boot-sucking mire. Once deep into her belly and past the muddiest bits, you could pause and recognize you were inside some sort of primeval cathedral. The passageway was much wider than the span of your arms and the walls of this triangular cave met nearly twenty feet above. At the far end, about sixty feet in, there's another sacred "v," a private cleft that mirrors the entrance above the ground. If you're thinking of the labia and the cervix tucked deep within the tunnel of the vagina, you're imagining it right.

At the time, of course, we were not talking about the anatomy of the goddess. Though entering this cave felt like an initiation into a deeper relationship with the divine feminine, we didn't really name it as such. I can only wonder whether this day will play a part in my daughter's becoming. I'll be satisfied if she carries a half-remembered story about the time her mom took her to that crazy place commonly known as the Cave of Cats and tells people, "It was really cool." Will she be called back there when she is a grown princess, looking to find the next concentric circle of herself? I can only hope she'll tell me if she does. Both so I can worry over the trip as my mother wasn't there to do, and so we can compare notes about the ways it totally *does* look like the birth canal of the Earth Goddess.

We decided to leave the cave rather suddenly when I pointed out how the little stalactites looked like teeth and Moira got spooked. (Oops... She was right. Stalactites are creepy. Plus, there are folktales from around the world that warn of the dangers of *vagina dentata*, the vagina with teeth. Such stories warned men to stay away from dangerous, unknown women and may even have helped prevent rape. I certainly didn't bring any of this up at the time, but I rather loved the geological poetry of it all. They say life imitates art, but it's all reflected in the earth, too.) My daughter and my cousin took the headlamp and crawled up and out the narrow exit. Turning off my phone's flashlight, I lingered for a few moments in the blackness, remembering that I was allowed to take the time, that I was allowed to put down the mantle of responsibility and be the pilgrim soul, just for a moment. This is when I met a dark goddess who told me to call her Mór.

This cave isn't just associated with the legendary Queen Medb. The oldest stories describe the long dark depths of Oweynagat as the "fit abode" of the goddess Morrígan.[4] Though often associated with the battlefield, this great dark queen holds sway over so much more than war and bloodshed. She is also a goddess of fertility. A shapeshifter, she is both sides of the Sovereign coin. She reminds us that life is worth defending and that death cannot be avoided. And in my solitary moments in the cave, the Morrígan whispered to me that she knew I had spent a life enamored by the

---

4 Edward Gwynn, trans., *The Metrical Dindshenchas*, Revised: Feb 3, 2011, https://celt.ucc.ie/published/T106500D.html.

light, with appearances, with the demands of seeing and being seen. She needed me to become as comfortable and nimble in the depths of the otherworld as I was in the spotlight of the everyday.

I've been having conversations with Celtic deities for years, so I wasn't surprised that there was a voice in my head offering spiritual counsel, but I was pleasantly surprised to meet this new messenger. Brigid, Ireland's famous goddess turned saint who appeared in that portentous tarot reading that convinced me to say yes to this trip, has long been my bright and shining guide. Mór was inviting me to approach this Sovereignty work in a new way. She was there to remind me that the magic we need, the magic that changes us, comes through when we're willing to explore the wild, untamed places, both in the natural world and within ourselves. Of course, Mór (like any divine guide who agrees to be part of the journey) had been walking beside me all along, just waiting for her moment and my receptivity. Now that I was aware of her, she'd never fully disappear into the shadows again. I'd take her home as a sort of fairy hitchhiker, and she'd take up residence inside me with the rest of the cast of gods and guides who illuminate my way.

You do not need to start chatting up Celtic goddesses to do this Sovereignty work, but you may find that divine help shows up more often as you walk this path toward spiritual and creative freedom. Whether I was aware of the presence of goddesses like Mór and her sister Brigid, they've been walking beside me and helping me awaken bit by bit from the very beginning. Years ago, long before I had heard of Oweynagat and only shortly after I rediscovered this concept of Sovereignty, some divine being sent me a vision, a sort of waking dream. Back then, it felt like a personal invitation. I am so grateful that it's time to invite others to come along with me. Read it, and then close your eyes and let yourself imagine yourself on the journey.

Meditation: The Cave of Initiation

You have been journeying for days or even weeks. You may have left home with a group of companions or set off alone on your own quest. Your skin and hair are thick with the grime of the roads and the forest paths. All of your belongings, the very few that you have, are wrapped in a pack under your cloak, the same cloak that serves as your bed and your shelter.

Weapons are lashed to your waist, your thigh, and strapped across your back. Open yourself to understand that weapons are not always a blade and a bow. You could carry a quill and ink, a collection of healer's herbs, a satchel of diapers and swaddling cloths, prophecies from your gods, or simply the overflowing matter of your own heart. These are dangerous times, for sure, but you are a warrior of a kind. You fight darkness with your own special medicine. You are awake to the calling to come as you are with the gifts that you have gathered so far in your journey.

The people who walk beside you now—it seems like there are hundreds. They speak in different dialects and come from different tribes, but you trust that you are united by a common purpose and that purpose creates peace. You have not walked this path before, yet you feel drawn and destined to see where it leads You walk this path with your blessed weapons in order to more deeply connect with your own power and craft.

Cutting down long slopes into a valley, you see other groups of travelers. All of you will walk along the riverbed until you reach the great cave just above the edge of the water on the western shore. You enter single file, and there is no worry about rank or order. There is trust. There is the call. Those who doubted the mission turned back long ago.

The corridor within the rock is narrow and low and dark, but again, there is trust. There is the knowledge deep within that you are entering the womb and that this is a place of safety, of revelation, of rebirth. There is light ahead. It is coming from a vent high above, yes, but the walls seem to cast their own glow as well. The air is warm and soft, and you feel like you're coming home.

You emerge from the tunnel and enter a great cavern, vaster than any enclosed space you have ever seen. Your people have no concept of "cathedral," but this is as great and soaring as any temple that will be built by human hands in the centuries to come.

At the center of this chamber is a deep blue pool, and at the center of that, a high rock reaching to the light above. A woman sits on a throne carved from that stone, whether by human hands or by the elements of this womb-cave, you cannot tell. You get down on one knee and bow your head, knowing that you will receive a blessing, trusting that all will become clear as each moment unfurls.

You and the rest of the visitors—warriors, sages, chieftains, mothers, healers—all form a ring around the edge of the pool. The woman at the center speaks and does not speak… This is a place where all stories are revealed but where so little needs to be said.

Rocks in the water, unnoticed until now, become her stepping-stones. She climbs down from her throne so she can walk amongst you and stand before each visitor in turn.

She places her hand on a bowed head. Then, she places her hands on shoulders and bids that person rise. She leans in close and whispers low in their left ear. You long to know what she will say to you. It seems that each visitor receives their own message. This is the voice of individual destiny.

When she reaches you and touches your head, you feel as if you've been opened up to taste the entire universe. You feel as if you have been purified and loved and seen and filled with inestimable knowledge. When she touches your shoulders, you feel as if you have been mothered and nourished and strengthened beyond measure. And when she whispers in your ear, you hear…

What? Pause and listen. Take her message into you. Let it illuminate the shadows within you and let her words guide your way.

She is the Sovereignty Goddess, the conveyor of power, of destiny. She is here to introduce everyone to their own gifts, their own cup of contribution. You and the Sovereignty Goddess are one and the same. You are being initiated into her circle not because you are meant to be her follower but because you are meant to become her in your own way.

You are a healer, a priestess, a revolutionary. You are a warrior, an artist, a sorceress. You are an agent of transformation who refuses to accept this world as is, who refuses to settle for the status quo. A force and source of Sovereignty, you begin by recognizing your own sacred right to heal, create, and love who you are, and then you can dance with your divine obligation to offer that magic to others.

The Sovereign woman does not rule for her own glory, and she does not do this work for the sheer sake of power. She becomes Sovereign so that she can teach this to others and empower everyone to heal, create, and love this world into its next evolutionary stage.

Now that you know all this, now that you know that you are being empowered to sit on your own throne, lean toward the goddess once again. Does she have another message for you? Perhaps it's your turn to share a message with her. Listen closely again. Speak if it feels like it's your turn.

When it is time for you to leave this cave, you will know it. You entered with a vast crowd, but now it is only you, ready to set out on your own quest. Return to the narrow tunnel, out into the open air beneath a vast sky.

Notice the world around you. Is it a bright sapphire day? Is the sun rising or setting? Are you called to begin this quest on a dark starry night or under the guidance of a full moon daring to peek through the clouds?

Begin to walk. Where is your first stop on this journey of Sovereignty? It doesn't have to be the moment of birth or the day you got your first period. It may seem like you're starting right in the middle of the story. In fact, you probably need to land yourself in the snarliest center of your Sovereignty story and work slowly toward the edges until you see that there was never a definitive beginning at all.

Writing Prompt: Upon Meeting a Sovereignty Goddess

This meditation is purposefully open-ended, full of questions for you to answer and designed so you can fill in the details. Tell your own story of visiting the mysterious Sovereignty Goddess.

- What "weapons" do you carry?
- What's your sense of the "common purpose" that brings you to the cave?
- What did the Sovereignty Goddess whisper to you?
- Are you a warrior, a sorceress, a chieftain, a mother, a healer, an artist, a sage? Explore every title that resonates with you and create your own, too.
- What did you say to the Sovereignty Goddess?
- Where is your first stop on your Sovereignty journey? Think about a key moment when you stepped into your own power and declared, "This is who I am and who I am meant to be." You may also be drawn to a moment when you were *not* Sovereign because you want to do the work of healing the past.

CHAPTER 3

The Indirect Path to Sovereignty

We live in a universe with mysterious origins, and I believe our souls endure long before birth and stretch long after death. When you think of it that way, beginnings aren't all they're hyped up to be. And yet, we storytellers and seekers of Sovereignty need to start somewhere. I invite you to come with me to a backyard on Cape Cod in July of 2010 when it felt like everything was beginning and ending at the same time.

On this particular Sovereign afternoon, in the company of a bold red cardinal, I said the words, "I am not coming back."

My mother was dead. We'd been embraced by the hundreds of people who'd come to her wake. We'd filled—and emptied—coolers full of beer as we hosted a huge gathering that felt more like the sixtieth birthday party we never got to throw her than her post-funeral reception. We'd gone to the beach to watch every sunset because it was the only thing we could count on each day now that she was gone and life would never be the same. We were just beginning the long lonely walk into the reality of living without her now that the crowds had thinned out and all that remained were the sympathy cards.

The rest of the family had gone back to their lives, too. My husband had gone back home to New York to work. My sister had returned to her Boston apartment to try to recreate some semblance of her old routine. But the baby and I stayed on. Moira must have been sleeping when I told my father I was going out to the backyard to use the phone. It was time. I'd been working up the courage to do this since the moment I heard the news.

The week before, my father had called early on a Tuesday morning just before I started the harried process that was packing up the diaper bag and heading to work. He said simply, "Your mother. She's gone." I had two thoughts nearly simultaneously, but I like to think "No, that's not possible" was the first. She was a healthy sixty-year-old woman still years from retirement. We had just seen her on Sunday. People in our family don't just drop dead of heart attacks. I was not meant to raise this baby without the support of the world's most dedicated grandmother.

"It can't be true" is the thought that was easy to speak aloud. It's what every abandoned child is supposed to say. The second thought needed to echo inside, a sonic thread I could cling to as we all struggled through the wildly impossible process of saying goodbye. But there it was, the only thought that offered even an ounce of comfort. *Now I can quit my job* became my mantra as we drove from our house in New York State back to my childhood home in Massachusetts.

I'm not sure when I shared this choice (which felt more like a command from the universe than a personal decision) with my husband and my father, but when I expressed it, I must have sounded unshakable. Perhaps in the midst of all the confusion and desperation, they just needed someone to be sure about something. Perhaps they just wanted to give someone something that they needed. Perhaps they realized they weren't going to force a grieving daughter to leave her own daughter just to earn a few grand a month. All I knew was that I had an infant to raise, a dad to keep company, and I couldn't go back to that windowless office where I had spent the last seven years. Suddenly, life was just too damn short and I couldn't spend one more day doing something I did not love. Ignoring the voice in my head that said, quite calmly, "don't go back" simply wasn't an option.

It's important to note that I was leaving a job as a junior manager at a prestigious liberal arts college library, not a uranium mine or a poultry processing plant. Though my desk sat in a depressing neon-lit box, the rest of the place was a castle complete with gargoyles and narrow stone staircases worn down by generations of scholars. But even as I was surrounded by books and progressive politics and "problems" rarely more urgent than a roof leak or a senior faculty member who was cranky about his study carrel, I felt trapped. Organizational goals were all brambled with personal alliances and conflicts. Instead of experiencing the kind of professional growth that takes you upward and outward, I was caught in a tangled root ball of privilege and petulance. I was assistant to the director of the library, the right-hand woman to the ruler of the palace. My position gave me keys to the great gothic tower that soared over campus and the chance to lord over a hundred student employees. Paid to be a princess, I was propelled by delusions of grandeur, court intrigue, and the crush of inexperience. I wore Banana Republic trousers rather than a gown, but the effect was the same. In theory, I had a million freedoms and there were chances to rise through the institutional ranks, but I just saw the endless lines of shelves, my similarly entitled and dissatisfied colleagues, and the perpetual cycle of students stumbling in and then flying off to explore the world while I stayed on to greet the next round of freshmen.

With Mom gone, I felt it was my duty as the oldest daughter to step into the role of matriarch. Quitting my job would be the final, decisive break with my princess self. Or so I thought. It felt like I was being forced to crown myself queen of my own life, whether I was ready or not. So I did. Kinda.

The Ragged Truth of a Sovereignty-Making Moment

Here's the thing about first acts of Sovereignty and life-changing, Sovereignty-making moments: Generally, they don't resemble empowered, vision-driven choices at all. In moments of crisis, the decisive power that is channeled through you often springs from a bubbling pool of pride and self-loathing, of fractured hope and barbs of fear, of intense love and deepest despair. You speak the words—*I quit, I'm leaving you, I'm starting again*—but the departure has only just begun. The choice was a long time coming and it will take time to adjust to the new reality created by your declaration of independence and personal power. It *is* possible to take a radical Sovereign step with a clear vision and an open heart, but you only learn how because you made those ragged-ass bids for Sovereignty back when you were an absolute mess. When you can come to understand a Sovereignty-making moment for what it is, then you can start making conscious moves toward your most Sovereign self with awareness and grace. Then again, as my stories will bear out, it can still be sloppy and difficult, even when you start to learn the lingo. Back there in the liminal space of fresh grief, I thought princesses and queens belonged in fairytales and I couldn't find much wisdom at all in this cruel world.

A new sort of terror was creeping in around the edges of loss. Suddenly, life was more fragile and brief than I had ever imagined. With only that maiden-mother-crone model to guide me, I didn't know how to proceed through life if there was no beloved elder to stand between me and the grave. When I put in my two weeks' notice, I would have told you I knew nothing of Sovereign courage. And, at the same time, thirty-one years of living and growing meant that I was a veteran of such terrain. Sovereignty-making moments occur throughout life, but we don't necessarily have the tools or the vocabulary to understand that. I couldn't see all the plot twists I'd already managed to navigate and the pain I'd survived. Perspective is something severely lacking in princesses, bless their hearts. The same is true for anyone caught in the cycles of trauma. Then again, it's also true for most humans much of the time. Now that I am more experienced at tracking just where I am in the Sovereignty Knot, I can sense when I am moving across the stage with the princess's eagerness and hesitation, the queen's confidence and authority, the wise woman's ease and insight. All those years ago, however, I was sure I was making it all up as I went along. I wasn't conscious of Sovereignty or archetypes. All I could do was exercise what little control I had now that I was a half-orphaned creature with a girl of my own to raise.

Grief Is a Gateway for Truth

At this point, I just want to rush my story forward to another July three years later when I started to understand this whole Sovereignty thing. But to do that, I would be forcing us across the crucible of grief, dismissing its damnable, transformative power. It would be nice to say that my emergence into some Sovereign version of myself was accomplished through a combination of meditation, self-compassion, and green smoothies. I tried all of those things, and I tried sheer willfulness, denial, whining to anyone who would listen, and bottles of wine, too. Ultimately, the only way over was through. I learned to walk across fresh shards of sorrow each day until the glass beneath my feet was ground back into soft sand that I could run and play on.

The quest for Sovereignty is enacted across the entire lifetime, so my own Sovereignty story certainly began well before my mother died and I quit that job. Any true Sovereignty story includes the shadows as well as the light, so I need to tell you about the days when I was most distanced from my sense of agency, power, and worth.

Fresh out of grad school, I realized there wasn't much you could do with a degree in Anglo-Irish literature and drama if you didn't have the confidence to pursue a PhD. Let me rephrase that. There wasn't much *I* could do with a master's degree when I didn't have any confidence at all, so I took a job as a receptionist at a gigantic orthopedic surgery firm in a Hartford, Connecticut high-rise. I'll never forget the secretary who seemed to want to point out my ineptitude by asking, "Aren't you the one who went to college?" My reply, "Actually, I'm the one who went to graduate school," stung me more than it stung her, of course. For a year, I kept returning to that hive of broken bones and broken spirits, unable to see that I had any other options at all.

I knew this wasn't the place for a Sovereignty Goddess to be. But I wasn't a divine being. I was a human female born with a congenital dental condition. I had cracked a couple of molars in my European travels, so I needed insurance to pay to get them fixed. Theoretically, my commitment to getting my teeth crowned was what forced me to go to that miserable office where two dozen male doctors ruled over a staff of one hundred women like a pack of petty kings. Could that really have been the only reason I felt so unable to find another job? Was that really why I put aside my degrees, my brains, and the work ethic I'd been honing since I was a kid scooping ice cream? I still don't fully understand the choices I made back then, but I know my body and soul were heavy with some kind of fear I could not name. Perhaps it had something to do with coming of age just as our illusions of safety and American exceptionalism collapsed with the Twin Towers, but I don't think this was a question of geopolitics. I was a creature who craved security and praise, and I couldn't figure out how to fit into a system that didn't hand out grades and scholarships. Without an ivory tower to hide in, I took the other option available to a princess: I fell into a pair of good strong arms.

There was a boy, of course. I'd rushed home from Ireland just after final exams to be with the guy who had invited me to live with him in a downtrodden corner of suburbia. Even now, I love the *idea* of that particular boyfriend, but no one could have cared for me enough to make up for my own lack of self-love. Except maybe my mom. Every chance I had, I climbed into my vintage powder-blue Ford Taurus (which, to add further insult to all this injury, was five years older than the Ford Taurus I had driven in high school) and drove up Interstate 84 to the Mass Pike. Back then, "road-trip magic" just meant that the car didn't break down on the way. I'd only take a full breath when I saw the bridge that would take me across the Cape Cod Canal.

I was born on my mother's twenty-ninth birthday under the sign of Gemini. She was my twin. She was my best friend. She only had a chance to live two-thirds of the life she deserved. At least I can say I chose to spend as much of her short life with her as I did. As the priest said at her funeral, she was both peace and passion and she lived until she died. Early in our marriage, my husband asked me, "Is it weird that I feel like one of my friends is coming into town when your mom comes to visit?" Not at all. She had that effect on everyone. My mom, Jeanine, or "Mammy" as my friends and I called her, was the kind of woman who would sit up late drinking with her daughter and her college roommates, but who always knew just when to leave the party. Mammy would dance all night at a wedding, surrounded by young groomsmen, but when the lights came on you'd realize she'd been inspired by pure love of the music and was more than capable of driving the tipsy princesses home.

Able to pull together a fantastic meal for six or eight at a moment's notice with the stuff she found in the corners of the fridge, my mother was the queen who cared for everyone who appeared in her castle. All of us could deal with the bullshit and the stress if we had her to take care of us, make us laugh, and pour us more champagne. We could put the quest for personal Sovereignty on hold when she was there to untangle the knots and hold all the loose ends. There were lots of reasons why I clung to princesshood for as long as I did—some of them had to do with privilege, some to do with my basic personality type, and some had to do with the fact that I didn't need to worry about being queen when we already had someone so fine to wear the crown.

You could say my mom was the empress of overcommitment, too. I rang her around noontime on the day I was in labor with Moira. Though I'd been up the whole night—my water broke just after midnight—I'd waited for the sun to rise to wake my husband and call Mammy. She said she would pack the car and be with us in just over four hours. Labor wasn't progressing—the baby wouldn't be born until after 5AM the next day—but I wanted my mother there to hold my hand. I was scared and excited and I thought I needed her beside me for whatever it was that lay before me.

"Hey!" I said, "Just calling to see how close you are."

"Oh," she said, "Nearly there." And then there was a brief silence and "Dammit, I forgot they were doing work on the bridge."

"The bridge over the Hudson, Mom? Oh good, you'll be here in a little over an hour." There was another silence. It was unclear if she was listening to me at all.

"Ugh. I guess I'll have to take the Bourne Bridge." My mother hadn't actually left the Cape yet, and that would mean she wouldn't get to us until late afternoon.

In her defense, she had things to do: She cooked my father a turkey and whipped him up a lasagna so he wouldn't starve in her absence. The so-called meals that my dad would pull together in his cold kitchen after she was gone still break my heart.

I cannot help but wonder how much of that spectacular caregiving came at the expense of my mother's Sovereignty. Not a writer, besides birthday cards, she only left one journal entry in a composition book from the early seventies and an unsent letter to her Lamaze coach describing my birth story. That was one more way she was so deeply and perfectly human—she *meant* to do so much for so many people, including herself. It's just that she gave nearly every ounce of energy she had to her parents, my dad, my sister, my husband, my baby girl, and me. What was left over went to the sick kids and the lonely little old ladies she visited as a respiratory therapist. Maybe I run the risk of canonizing my mother. I'm not sorry about that. Even though I know full well that she was far from the perfect blend of princess, queen, and wise woman, she did a damn good job embodying love.

I do think my mom's princess game was near flawless. In her fifties, she walked this nearly impossible line of being one of the girls while also managing to be the grown up in the room. And she was a gutsy, accomplished princess when she was young, too. Her parents couldn't even think of paying for her to go to college, so she put herself through Northeastern University with the proceeds from her co-op jobs. She studied political science back when few girls pursued anything other than teaching or nursing. The summer before she graduated, she fell in love with a bartender she met when she was a waitress at a Cape Cod bar. After a long-distance courtship and then a shared six-month adventure across the country, she and my dad would get married in the same small town where they met and she'd live on that little peninsula for the rest of her days.

When it came to being queen, her realm was a small one. Not a risk-taker, she wouldn't let her own dreams pull stronger than those of her family, but she didn't seem to be someone who minded. She thought of going to social work school because she felt like the best part of her in-home healthcare work wasn't setting people up with nebulizers and sleep apnea kits, but with sitting and talking to them, holding their stories and holding their hands. I'm not sure how deep the dream went or how much it cost her to let it go. Surely it seemed impossible for her to go to Boston College for her Master of Social Work when her daughters were there, each needing $100,000 to get their own bachelor's degrees.

If she were still here, we'd talk about my kids and the kids who were separated from their parents at the southern border. She and I were impassioned kitchen table revolutionaries, talking about every outrage and every progressive cause we could believe in. And yet, my mother wasn't always completely at home in her wise woman self. Her fixation on "let's keep it light" and "don't worry, be happy" meant that difficult emotions were generally discouraged. There was a lot she refused to feel and didn't want us to feel. I'm not sure what she would think of these Sovereign archetypes of mine. When I was first exploring earth-based religions and Celtic spirituality, she would come with me to seasonal rituals at the local New Age shop, but my world wasn't hers. She had the Church of her childhood, which she picked at like a consummate cafeteria Catholic. With the rare exception of a few Caroline Myss books, Mom barely dipped a toe into the personal development waters. Her second-wave feminism and her passion for liberal politics were so ingrained in her that she rarely seemed to think about it. Programmed to be practical, her attention was focused on current events at home, at work, at the beach, at Fenway Park, and on MSNBC.

Who would my mother have been if she'd been raised to expect a bit more, if she'd had the advantages that would have inspired her to invest more fully in her own dreams? I only get to ask these questions because she is gone, of course. If she were here, I would just be able to watch her in motion and I wouldn't have time or reason to worry that she was supposed to be more than she was. Perhaps I could stop confusing my goals with hers. If she were here I could ask her to help me as I frantically rushed forward to accomplish the next thing. Perhaps I could listen to her when she told me that this moment itself was enough.

If she were still here to be the queen, tending to all of us and keeping us all knit tightly together, there would be no need to wonder about everything that didn't unfold for her. If we look to the life she lived and loved as evidence, it's clear that *we* were her living dream. At some level, we knew that when she was here with us, but once she was gone, who would dream us into being?

Once she was gone, we had to create and live our own Sovereign dreams.

Here's the impossible piece, the piece that proves that this whole Sovereignty undertaking is as terrible as it is beautiful, and that Sovereignty is as likely to tie us up in knots even as it sets us free. I *needed* my mother, my best friend in the whole wide world who was destined to be the greatest grandmother the universe had ever seen. And, at the very same time, it was only with her death that I could fully inhabit my own life.

Hold on a second here. I am not suggesting that there's some grand succession plan here. As I said before, I did not actually become the matriarch of our family just because the throne was vacated. We Gen-Xers and millennials do not need to wait for the baby boomers to pass on before we can get a chance to become Sovereign in our own lives. Instead, I'm saying that in the face of loss, I had a chance to see myself fully. She wasn't there to hold a lamp or to cast a shadow, and so I had to see myself as I was—a mostly oblivious princess with some of the trappings of the queen and occasional moments of a wise woman's insight.

Now, I'm deeply grateful for all of the ways I've learned to stand Sovereign in my own life, but I wouldn't trade being a well-loved daughter for anything in the world. That's the foundation that I still rely upon today. We need sheroes who can hold us as we grow. We need the shelter of home when it feels necessary to retreat from the cruel world. We need these things, but only some of us get them, I know. I think it's true that every mother does her best, but, sometimes, a mother's "best" looks abusive and monstrous because she suffered abuse at the hands of monsters. My own access to mother love becomes part of the medicine I can offer when I hold healing space for the daughters of women who didn't know how to show love. When a daughter rises from the ashes of a broken relationship with her mother, she can reclaim her voice and discover a sense of Sovereignty that feels safe, healthy, and whole.

The Princess Awakens

Three years after Mom died, I was sitting on the front steps watching a summer day ease by. As was typical during that time, I was feeling anything but relaxed. My daughter held a stick of sidewalk chalk in each hand, happily drawing stick people princesses and kitty cats. Suddenly, something just clicked and I had words for the feelings of helplessness and stuckness that had pervaded my life.

In a horrifying rush, I determined that I *was* a princess. Leaving my unsatisfying job and making my great bid for Sovereignty actually made me more beholden to others—particularly men—than I had been since I finished school. For all my fierce dedication to feminism and my struggle to prove my capabilities and my worth, I was wholly dependent on my husband and my dad. As a new mom who didn't have much of a local community beyond my former workplace, I had grown increasingly reliant on those guys for emotional support, too. In the years of mourning, motherhood, and still unsuccessful bids at creating a new professional life, I had completely lost the connection to my own power.

When I left the job at college, it wasn't just to grieve and attend mommy-and-me classes. During maternity leave, I had started to dream up a side gig that I hoped would catch me when I eventually made the well-considered move from salaried safety into the mystery of self-employment. I'd fantasized about building a creative career for as long as I could remember, but the reality of working for myself was remarkably less glamorous than I had imagined. I would turn out to be the world's most demanding, unpredictable boss; the hours were lousy and the pay was even worse. Years into my entrepreneurial adventure as a copywriter and a social media marketer, I was barely making enough money to cover groceries and childcare. Money had become the third rail in our marriage, so my husband stressed about the bills in silence—except for the tremendous explosions of frustration and worry that ended with me weeping with the same kind of wounded heartbreak I suffered at my mom's graveside. We got by thanks to help from my dad, my grandfather, my uncle, and the bit of money from my half of my mother's retirement fund. I felt like a failure and I was drowning in both hopelessness and resentment, feeling like I needed to make money to prove my worth and despising the capitalist system that made it so.

Money isn't necessarily essential to Sovereignty. It is possible to have personal, creative, and spiritual Sovereignty even if you do the unpaid work of caregiving while another member of the household focuses on bringing in the dough. In our case, however, we had a two-income mortgage and only one income. Theoretically, I had the freedom I'd longed for, but it wasn't sustainable and the dance with credit card debt meant we never felt safe. The financial issues were a symptom rather than the cause of my anxiety. I'd fallen into patterns of victimhood and lost track of my resilience and my own self-reliance. Though I'd never loved my career, I hadn't realized how it had been an important source of Sovereignty. In my escape from the nine-to-five, I lost something I hadn't yet learned how to value.

It would take longer than I ever expected to translate my early stumbles as a freelancer into the creation of a writing community and a coaching business. In part, that's because I was a full-time mom and because I had a great deal of emotional healing to do, of course. In part, it's because entrepreneurship is hard—especially when you're not a natural businesswoman. Finding the right work would enable me to step into my Sovereignty. And yet—here's another paradox inherent to this whole Sovereignty Knot endeavor—I needed to be Sovereign in order to create the conditions in which I would create such a world for myself.

The Source of Sovereignty

When I recognized just how far I had drifted from personal and creative Sovereignty, I only had a limited vocabulary. Instantly, I labeled myself a foolish, spoiled princess. Back then, my only goal was to be a queen. When, at well past the age of thirty, I realized that neither marriage, motherhood, nor home ownership would come with a crown, I was devastated. As you'll see in the next chapters, my understanding of Sovereignty would shift and change. I would realize that the princess had many magnificent qualities I would want to retain and I would see that being queen wasn't necessarily as fabulous as I expected, but I wasn't there yet. On that particular day amongst my daughter's chalk drawings, I was just too full of shock, guilt, and self-reproach. I was a mom and a wife. I was working every day (albeit without a ton of success), and I'd consistently had a job since I was twelve years old. And still, I felt powerless and rudderless. I couldn't feel the earth beneath my feet or trust myself to make the next right choice.

Over time, I would realize that even if I was a princess, no one was going to save me. Sovereignty always has been something you need to achieve for yourself. My mom never would have presented me with a crown. It wasn't because she died too soon or because she wasn't Sovereign enough to pass on the gift. It's not a mother's job to initiate her daughter in some mighty queen-making ceremony. Instead, Sovereignty is conveyed in a million small ways. It happens during potty training and the introduction of solid foods. It happens during real, brave discussions about intimacy, booze, and drugs. In my experience, mothers teach Sovereignty lessons when they take their daughters to campaign for candidates who support civil rights, gay rights, trans rights, and women's rights (my mom had me carrying signs for our congressional representative Gerry Studds when I was five). Mothers inspire Sovereignty when they support their daughters' decisions to study what makes them most passionate and to give birth at home. Sovereignty develops when mothers allow their daughters to fail and flail while being fully themselves, and then welcome them home with open arms.

My mom did many of those for me, but when she left so early and so unexpectedly, I was forced to do it alone. It took me a while to pick up the shattered pieces and begin to create my own new Sovereign story that was about integration and wholeness. I had no choice now that Mom wasn't there to hold everything together.

My life would almost certainly look vastly different if my mom were here and I could return to that house I grew up in. Imagining my mother's unrealized dreams isn't a constructive or healing exercise and neither is wondering what life would be like if she were still here. It's a matter of speculative fiction that brings little comfort and even less truth. I know Mammy would be proud of me now. She'd be excited about the community of writers I've gathered together and about this book. She'd be most proud of her granddaughters. This Sovereignty work probably would have come into the world in a slightly different form, and I'm not quite sure how much we'd talk about its development. There is one thing I know for sure: Mom would have *hated* the way I first formulated my recipe for Sovereignty.

On that fateful day sitting on the front steps when I was thirty-four, I looked in the mirror—or rather, I looked at the screen while taking a selfie—and saw a princess and realized she was *me*. I had only one response: kill.

Writing Prompt: A Sovereignty-Making Moment

This chapter covers a lot of territory, crisscrossing over more than a decade of my life as I blindly embodied and then, eventually, began to acknowledge the princess within me.

Two themes emerge most strongly: grief and work. They may seem unrelated, but here's what they really have in common: Both have a way of testing your Sovereignty, revealing your Sovereignty, and building your Sovereignty. (And they both have a way of showing the ways in which you're *not* standing in your Sovereignty, too.)

Look to your own life in search of a Sovereignty-making moment. It probably came at a moment of great transition, either something you chose or something that seemed to just happen to you. Write into that experience, noticing the ways you did and did not stand in your own power. As ever, lead with compassion. You'll notice the last line in this chapter—"I had only one response: kill." I hope you'll avoid such self-directed anger, but if you notice that coming through, be honest with yourself. Honesty is the first step in healing.

CHAPTER 4

Free the Princess

For you, daughter, there is no blame,
For you no portion of guilt,
For you're made in my likeness.
You can take the crucifixion from your voice.
I will stroke your forehead til you sleep,
Til you pass over into the dreamworld
Where we can walk together in gardens wet with rain
Or fly along old star roads
Or sit quietly near running water

—From *"The Ghost of My Mother Comforts Me"*
by Paula Meehan[5]

---

5 Paula Meehan, *Pillow Talk* (Loughcrew, Ireland: Gallery Press, 1994) 38.

Originally, I was enraptured by the phrase "slay the princess, crown the queen." The wise woman wasn't even part of that run-on sentence in those early days. Clearly, she wasn't. The wise woman knows that nothing ever dies; it simply changes to assume a new form.

When I did find the words "free the princess," I was still a long way from giving myself permission to do so. Once I detected that princess energy inside me, I would wrestle with every kind of self-recrimination. How could I be one of "those people"? Princesses are for people who never outgrow the Disney definition of womanhood. Princesses are for people who can name the Kardashians. Princesses are for people who really, really like pink and keep perfect homes. Princesses are pawns of the patriarchy. They are selfish and close-minded and judgmental. Oh, wait... Oh, damn. I actually kinda like *Frozen* and love how Moana breaks the mold and fits right in with the Disney pantheon. I may not be much of a housekeeper or have an eye for interior design, but I would love a nice clean house to store my boots (if not my glass slippers). Yes, there was a princess both thriving and cowering inside me. There still is, but hopefully I embody her power rather than her weaknesses now that I understand more about how this whole Sovereignty thing works.

Looking back, the princess's patterns, both positive and unhealthy, were written all over my life. A propensity for experimentation, boldness, and optimism? That was me. A vivid imagination paired with a desire to see, know, and explore new terrain and new philosophies? Absolutely. Did my wild embrace of my sexuality occasionally become destructive bids for attention and affection? Yep. Did my lust for adventure turn around on itself to become paralysis in the form of escapism (hello, Netflix) or in fear of the unknown (hello, underemployment)? Hell, yeah. And does looking back on my intense and wearying days as a princess going full tilt make me feel both heady nostalgia and scalding shame? You better believe it.

Since the chronic diminishment of self-worth is so common in women in our society and the system is rigged to make it so, it's all too easy to look back on everything, both the messy mistakes and the glittering moments, and blame the princess for doing it wrong. She's the first one to be indoctrinated in the too much/not enough double bind that has been inflicted on and internalized by just about all of womankind. It's the princess in us that's enraptured by the diet culture and most at risk in the rape culture. On the positive side, my experiences bumming around the great museums of Europe and attending slam poetry sessions in dank basements in my early twenties have shown me that the princess often has the freedom to access actual "culture," too.

It's been easy to look at my brash, young, outspoken self—in high school I was voted "most likely to speak her mind"—and cringe. Squinting my eyes at my college self, I can see all the ways I kept my head down and studied hard and sacrificed my voice. It's easy to look past the good grades and lament the lost opportunity. When I peer through the haze to what's left of my memories of drunken nights and think about all the near misses—whether the stairs I didn't fall down or the guys who didn't actually assault me—my palms still get sweaty. When I consider the stupid jobs I took and how they set the tone for an accidental sort of professional life, I sigh. When I look back at that enormously expensive wedding, I kind of want to bury my head in the sand of the beach where we didn't actually get married (it poured and the ceremony was held inside). That great big party was the pinnacle of my princessery, though I did resist the tiara. In part, I got swept up in the matrimonial-industrial complex, but you'll understand more about why I was so desperate for pomp and ceremony when I tell you a bit more about my love story later on.

There's just so much to regret. And I know full well how fortunate I was to be a white girl being afforded every opportunity to make the most of my life. I was so damn fortunate, I had the luxury of sloshing my bucket of potential as I hurried along because I trusted that I could get a refill at any time. And if I try to put any of this in the safe, hallowed place of the past tense, please kick me under the table and make me tell everyone why I yelped in pain. The princess abides. The princess within persisted well after I started doing all the grown up things and even after I began to do the Sovereignty work that would make it possible for me to embody the queen and the wise woman on a regular basis. The princess giggles and snorts, struts and drops shit everywhere every damn day of my life. It has taken a long time to say this, but finally I can: The princess still thrives within me. And as I realize Sovereignty is about embracing all parts of the self, I can tell you that I wouldn't ask my princess to be anyone other than who she is.

Sovereignty is about more than being Queen of Everything. The goal is not to leave princesshood behind. Instead, Sovereignty is about integration. To be Sovereign is to accept and move through all the archetypes across all parts of life. To be Sovereign is to stand at the center of your own life, confidently able to embody all that you are. But as with so many things related to Sovereignty, this is easier to say than it is to do.

Not so long ago, I looked back on my thirties and dared to refer to the period as my "lost decade." Over those ten years I became a mother, learned how to live without a mother, became a mother again, built a business, held a marriage together, and wrote a book. To dismiss all that is a seriously princessy thing to do. When I repudiate my own history, I only prove that I'm a little less worldly and wise than I would care to admit. The princess gets lost in the comparison game. She's easily enraptured by the myth of scarcity that says, "All the stuff I accomplished and survived would count more if only I had also managed to…" (You fill in the blank with whatever it is that would make you "worthy" of the crown: making six figures, losing the baby weight, running for the school board, organizing a voter drive, managing to put on makeup and cook organic meals every night despite all the demands, exhaustion, and pain.) The more we achieve and the more we look like the woman in charge, the tougher this sense of "not enoughness" can be. Because here's the funny thing (that's not really all that funny): The more we discover about the princess, the more we learn about this archetype; and the more we come to terms with how she works in our lives, the more likely we are to revile her. That makes her shadow loom larger than ever. And that makes it too hard to say yes when the princess invites you dancing and declares that it's time to take off the pajamas and start glowing in the dark.

When I dismissed my thirties as a wasted decade, I could only see the opportunities I hadn't pursued. I rolled my eyes at all my dopey, unfulfilled dreams and they loomed like failures rather than roads not taken. Thoughtlessness, shortsightedness, and a general lack of empathy are the limitations of the princess. Here I was, blaming the princess within me for living out her natural patterns of experimentation, play, adventure, and optimism. I was using the princess's own qualities to shame myself. I would look at all the big stuff I hadn't done (because the "little stuff" like healing grief and child-rearing got in the way) and just saw evidence that I couldn't fulfill my lofty princess hopes or keep up with the queen's insatiable demands. Sometimes, I would be able to notice all the ways I avoided reality—in my home, my bank account, my community, this country, and this world—and I would just despise myself for holding tight to my advantages, my immaturity, and my refusal to become one of the grown-ups in the room.

Here's what I needed to spend several years figuring out: When I'm able to stand in my Sovereignty, to use the compassionate power of the queen beside the insight of the wise woman, I am able to see all of the ground I *did* cover. I see all the alliances I did build, all the laughter I did bring into the world, all the love I did make and share, and all the creative energy I did generate and manifest. I am able to forgive the princess and see her magnificence radiating more boldly than any of her perceived failures.

Once my mom was gone, I felt as if I was wandering the world alone. Though plenty of people did show up and offer what they could—as healers, as maternal figures, as friends—I was so caught up in grief and the ghostly weight of scarcity that I could only see such support as a sort of counterfeit mother love. Eventually, enough waves of sadness and healing would crash upon my beach to dissolve the dunes of isolation I had created for myself. I would be able to see that I had been establishing a vast network of supporters and kindred spirits who would never replace my mother, but who could hold me in the way that I needed as I started a new voyage.

The wise women I've welcomed into my life—and plenty of the smart men, too—have heard the stories I have told over the last decade and have begged me to stop being so hard on myself. They cringe not at my past mistakes, but at the cruelty I aim at my former self and at my tendencies to slip into "princess mode." I'll say this before one of my mentors or allies needs to say it to me: Brutally dismissing the girl and the woman I've been is probably the most hurtful thing I could do to my mother. After all, Mammy was the one who loved that girl completely, from the first flutter in her womb all the way through to those few precious months when she watched me love my own daughter into being. She adored who I was—passionate and carefree, self-focused and bighearted all at once. When I was hanging out with my mom and fully embodying my princess self, I gave Mammy permission to access her own freedom and passion. Follow the curve of the Sovereignty Knot a bit further: When I am fully in my princess self, I give my daughters permission to access their freest, most passionate parts, too.

Finally, I've begun to believe the people who've invited me to stop criminalizing my younger self. Finally, I have made some peace with the woman I was at twenty and thirty and just ten minutes ago. At last, I can stop asking my past self to be someone she was not ready to be. When I dare to remember anything from my past (and as a writer and healer who uses my own life as my laboratory, that's every day), I am learning how to acknowledge and love—and ultimately set free—my princess. And it's happening just in time, because my daughters need a Sovereign mama who loves who she is now and who she was then. I need to integrate all these aspects of myself so I can accept my girls as they start getting twisted in the Sovereignty Knot themselves. They are ten and five now; I should probably acknowledge that they are well on their way already because, as we established at the start of this book, these identities are not bound to age. The princess is the birthright of every woman, of every person who is willing to acknowledge the wild, playful, in-process imperfect feminine energy within.

A Princess, a Goddess, and a Saint

Tom Cruise is responsible for my passion for Ireland. And, back when I was a full-time princess, he sort of saved my life.

When I was thirteen, I would miss weeks of school at a time with a mystery illness. My mother was convinced it was the air quality at the middle school, but once I got to college and learned the word "depression," that mystery was solved. At the time, I wasn't particularly concerned with the cause. All I knew was that I wasn't much interested in living and there only seemed to be one cure: a VHS tape of *Far and Away*.

Every human born in Ireland intrinsically despises this movie's "Oirish" accents and most everyone else rolls their eyes at this film's early nineties epic flare, but I wasn't ashamed to love what I loved back in 1992. Tom Cruise was the biggest star on the planet, Scientology was barely on the radar screen, and no one saw the whole couch-jumping thing coming. I was a girl in love with a fantasy prince (who happened to be an impoverished Irish tenant farmer) and I had just discovered my fantasy island.

Eventually, I'd give the VCR a break and look beyond American movies to understand the country and the culture that seemed to be calling me home. A couple of years later, I would choose my confirmation name and it would be Bridget, honoring both my great-grandmother and the saint whose story is so core to Irish myth and identity. Though I couldn't know this as a fifteen-year-old Catholic kid, that name would serve me well on what would become a lifelong spiritual adventure.

Brigid (there are many ways to spell her name) is both a Pagan goddess and a Christian saint. Then and now, she was the perfect patron for me, her stories all spun with earthy mysticism and a passion that the Church could not tame. As Mary Condren says in *The Serpent and the Goddess*, "Layers of separate traditions have intersected, making Brigit out to be one of the most contradictory figures in Irish history."[6] This, of course, makes her the perfect character to help us navigate the Sovereignty Knot, particularly the contradictory territory of the princess.

Though the Christians are often credited with pushing the Goddess to the edges of Irish culture and belief, worship of the Great Mother had been suppressed by waves of invading hoards long before the Father, Son, and Holy Ghost entered the scene. And yet, the divine feminine was still a force in Ireland, so when St. Patrick and his proselytizing friends arrived, they needed to reckon with the holy women who came before. There was one particular Mother Goddess who had been trampled by centuries of invasion, but still endured. Ultimately, when the Church met the legacy of the Goddess Brigid, they took the only option available to them: They claimed her as their own.

---

6 Mary Condren, *The Serpent and the Goddess* (San Francisco: Harper & Row, 1989) 55.

The only way we know about Brigid as a goddess is through the weird, wild, and wonderful stories recorded by the Church in various volumes called the "Lives of Saint Brigit."[7,8] These records reveal that Brigid was associated with fire, healing, hospitality, poetry, beer, smithcraft, and fertility. The early documents of the Church also tell of how Brigid performed an abortion and protected women from rape. All this, of course, was left out of whatever sanitized pamphlet about the saints we used to pick our new holy names. Clearly, the princess inside me had a second sense for rebellion and badassery.

Brigid Claims Her Sovereignty

Fadó fadó … (Translation: long, long ago… that's the Irish equivalent of "once upon a time.")

Back in the days when the pagans mixed with the priests and the stories of Jesus and his miracles were fresh and new, there lived a young Irish girl named Brigid. She was the daughter of a slave woman, but her father was a powerful druid, and the prophecies foretold that she'd be more powerful still.

Though she was born into the Old Ways that were as old as the rocks and hills, the stories say that the Church laid claim to the girl's heart from the very beginning. And it seemed that she was inclined to love the Church right back. From the start, the young Brigid took a stand for her own Sovereignty. She decided early that she'd save her virginity for God.

---

7 Donnchadh Ó hAodha, trans., *Bethu Brigte*, Revised Sept 7, 2008, https://www.ucc.ie/celt/published/T201002/index.html. This mostly Irish language text probably dates from around 800, although an original version may have been earlier. It exists in one manuscript, Rawinson B 512, ff. 314-35v.
8 Whitley Stokes, trans., *On the Life of St. Brigit*, Revised June 14, 2013, https://celt.ucc.ie//published/T201010/index.html.

The men of her family knew she was keen to defend her chastity and become a nun, but when a wealthy man came to ask for her hand—she'd already performed a few miracles and word was getting around—her brothers hoped to convince her to marry. There was a hefty bride-price on the line, and no doubt they were thinking of how they could increase their herds, for this sister of theirs was surely worth a good few milk cows.

One brother in particular, Beccán, had strong opinions about how his sweet sister should spend her life. He looked into her sky-blue eyes and declared, "You've got such pretty eyes, sister. What a waste to spend each day closing them in prayer."

Brigid raised one brow, surprised that her brother would have such tender words for her. Just the night before, there had been a great debate about the marriage proposal. Her father and his sons were adamant, declaring that they couldn't turn down a fortune just for the sake of one girl's silly pious dreams.

Beccán went on, "No matter. Those pretty blues will close upon a husband's pillow soon enough."

"Son of the Virgin," Brigid said under her breath. For her, such an oath was a prayer.

"Dear brother, is it my eye you need to please that man who asks to marry me?" She pressed a steady finger to the corner of her right eye until it popped from its place and hung loose and terrible on her cheek. "Here, then, is that pretty eye for you," she said, "Though I can scarcely believe a man such as he would want a blind girl for a bride."

In the same instant, Beccán's own eye burst from its socket. Their brothers came down the path a moment later. They took no notice of Beccán's muffled shriek but rushed in to rescue their poor, wounded sister. They panicked when they realized there was no water to wash the wound. Ever calm, ever Sovereign, Brigid looked to her youngest brother. "Here," she said, "Take my staff, cut from the oldest oak, and press it into the sod just there." A fresh, clean stream bubbled up from the earth.

With a few drops of the healing water in her hand, she scooped her eye back into her head where it shone with as much light and beauty as it ever had. She immediately set off to keep her afternoon appointment with the priests down the lane but flashed a look at her wounded brother over her shoulder as she went. "And Beccán," she said in a voice that was much gentler than her words, "I do curse you and all your descendants. And I shall take that other eye into the bargain." With that, her bullying brother lost his sight completely and crumpled in a heap beside the stream of healing water that would never offer him any comfort or release.

Their father, Dubthach, appeared just then. Taking in the scene, he suddenly understood that a twisted sort of miracle had just taken place. Recognizing that his daughter's magic was not his to control, he declared, "Take the veil, my daughter. We bless you as you walk your holy path and will do no more to bar your way."

Brigid stopped and turned to look at her father. All she said before she set off again toward the church was, "Thanks be to God."

If I had the opportunity to read this story of Brigid when I was a high school kid, I would have missed the point. Certainly, I was a modern princess who was more obsessed with losing my virginity than I was worried about holding onto it. By the time I was reading translations of Irish manuscripts as an undergrad, I had long since left the Church. I was totally dedicated to finding the goddessy bits and merely skimmed anything related to Christianity. Focused on sex and paganism as I was, this story's provocative power would have been lost on me. It's too bad as this story of Sovereignty actually fit perfectly with the kind of princess I have always wanted to be.

Now, when I read this story of a young Brigid who refuses to lose herself to marriage vows, I'm utterly smitten with her divine combination of reckless sass and sacred devotion. It speaks directly to the princess's desire to say, "Don't mess with me," as well as her abiding longing to be *good*. And damn, it puts Brigid right in line with the cutting edge of the counterculture. In her time, Christianity was a new, disruptive force. To decide to go off and join the priests with their written language and their quiet rituals would have been a radical act in a culture that had long been dominated by warriors. It's hard to imagine it now after all these centuries of religious domination and repression, but as Mary Condren tells it, the early Church was actually a haven for women victimized by a brutal patriarchal society. Only the most Sovereign and self-assured women would find the courage and the conviction to leave the religion of their fathers in order to join the rebellious new religion that had just rolled into town.

Meet Your Princess

So what about your princess? Who was she then and who is she now? Do you allow your princess archetype to emerge and lead the way from time to time?

To fully embrace your princess energy, you're being asked to do magic on both sides of time. Make peace with who you are now in order to embrace with who you were then. Make peace with who you were then in order to welcome all you are now. And it doesn't end at some level of resigned acceptance. You're being asked to *celebrate* the way you embodied the princess once upon a time and how you still let her dance through your soul.

It's not necessarily going to be easy. You're going to need to reckon with all the patriarchal bullshit that is slut-shaming and ageism and all the indignities layered on women in between. You also need to penetrate your own batshit crazy beliefs that tangle you in regret and dissolve the ingrained habit of apologizing for all the ways you think the princess within you has been too little and too much.

I did not become the queen the moment my mother died nor the moment I quit my job nor even when I realized I did not want to be a princess anymore. As you'll remember, that was never the point. Instead, I became just a little bit Sovereign in every moment that I allowed myself to forgive and even celebrate the foolish bits of me that might have seemed easiest to disown. And I become a hell of a lot more Sovereign every time I throw my head back with ecstatic joy and just revel in this crazy-ass miracle of being alive.

When I am in touch with my princess energy, I can fully embrace my freedom, potential, vitality, physicality, boldness, innocence, sexuality, awakening, imagination, play, adventure, and optimism. And, when I slip into the unhealthy patterns that I never seem to fully outgrow—like low self-esteem, lack of self-worth, chronic neediness, bingeing, self-centeredness, victimhood, escapism, and fear of the unknown—I can see them for what they are. I can call in the energy of the queen and the wise woman to help me get back on solid ground.

There are no quick "hacks" that will help you ditch the negative habits and embody the healthy ones. You can't check a few items off a list to swiftly improve your Sovereignty score. All you can do is get curious, get loose, and begin to make this princess energy part of your life—and practice a heck of a lot of forgiveness and allow for plenty of celebration along the way.

The Princess Considers Forgiveness

Put simply, forgiveness is a tricky beast. By that, I don't mean that it isn't necessary and lovely in the right circumstances. I just mean that it's terribly easy to lose your Sovereignty in the forgiveness quest. There's a sort of secular gospel of forgiveness out there that makes us feel like we're putting our own health and sanity in jeopardy if we're not willing to pass out forgiveness like a hostess gives out after-dinner mints.

Before you start to consider how your own Sovereignty depends on forgiveness, you need to be clear that the forgiveness in question is yours to offer up. Terrible as the latest mass shooting may be, it's not up to you to forgive the man with the guns unless (goddess forbid) you or someone you love was a victim. (You can have plenty of other emotions in these situations, but don't waste your energy on forgiveness.) If you *have* personally been wronged, however, forgiveness doesn't have to be immediate or inevitable. The question is whether you have reached a point at which forgiveness is authentic and appropriate. As one of my teachers has helped me understand, it is only time to offer forgiveness when you have healed from the harm you've suffered. To simply slather the forgiveness balm on an oozing wound is to court denial and perpetuate the "smile pretty and practice some spiritual bypassing" madness that's created our culture of abuse.

Can forgiving the bastard who left you at the altar heal the hurt of abandonment? Sure, it's all part of the mix. But simply forcing yourself to turn the other cheek and practice some manufactured beneficence in the face of injury is more likely to make you a suffering phony than a Sovereign woman. To heal the deep wounds that come from loss, abuse, and ruptured relationships, you need to involve the entire self, not just the princess who feels the hurt most acutely.

The sort of forgiveness that we're talking about right now, the kind that frees the princess, is the self-directed kind. And to be even more specific, the kind of forgiveness that needs to be applied to acts of self-harm.

Writing Prompt: Forgiveness

Spend a bit of time with just what it is you need to forgive yourself for. Maybe you need to forgive yourself for starving yourself, for forcing yourself to purge, or for eating things that you knew would hurt you. Maybe you need to forgive yourself for drinking yourself into alcohol poisoning or for taking the drugs that took you on a bad trip. Maybe you need to forgive yourself for abandoning a friend who

---

needed you. Maybe you need to forgive yourself for staying too long in an abusive relationship.

Be specific. Be honest. Be aware of whether this is a familiar pain you've been holding onto, unforgiven for years, or whether you're just gathering the courage to name this thing as a form of self-harm you need to heal.

You may find yourself creating a long list of things both big and small that require self-forgiveness. You might feel called to tell the story of something that has seemed like an unforgivable act. Meet your truth on the page and then meet yourself with the spirit of forgiveness.

The Princess Considers Celebration

Once upon a time, I wanted to slay the princess. I wanted to entomb her in my early twenties and make her stay there with all my unexamined regrets. But to do so would rob me of the ecstasy and adventure that the princess wants to enjoy her whole life through.

The princess within knows how to laugh, how to flirt, how to set aside the worries and the deadlines to simply be here in this moment. The princess knows how to sneak in the backstage entrance and how to stay up talking until dawn. She knows how to stay up all night long making love, too. You probably need her more now than you did at twenty-one, when the whole world was designed to invite you to the party. You're invited to consider how you might celebrate the princess you once were. This is also a chance to allow the princess that's always been within you to bring more lighthearted energy into your daily life.

Writing Prompt: Celebration

Dare to remember the younger version of you who was wild, willful, and carefree (at least some of the time). Whether she was at the center of the social circle or someone who knew how to let her hair down when she was with a trusted few, explore those half-remembered details.

Explore the princess energies that were present in you back in the day. Consider what it would be like to celebrate moments in your life with that same kind of passion. What part of your princess self wants to be remembered?

And then, spend time writing about the princess energies that are still present in you today. Perhaps you're in a phase when you're making out and making love all the time. Maybe you access your princess energy when your heart leaps at the sight of a rainbow. Celebrate your adventurous spirit and your unbridled joy in whatever form it takes right now.

The Territory of the Princess

The princess's territory is the cliff. These are the hinterlands, the place between the wilds and the known world. These are the places that call to us, no matter our age, but particularly as young women trying to find our way. These are places that you must explore on your own, but paradoxically, these are the places you also wish to share with those you love. That's part of the mystery of the princess—she has so much to figure out on her own about her own life, but, at the same time, she's a social creature who needs companions to act as her mirrors and her foils.

I grew up playing hide and seek in Cape Cod's dunes, pretending I lived in a kingdom of white sand and beach grass, but it was up on Prince Edward Island in the Canadian Maritimes where I fully entered into relationship with nature for the first time. It's where the adventure began and where I first heard the call of the cliffs. On the island, the earth is a rainbow of red, from the rich rust soil to the faded rose beaches. At the end of the green fields of potatoes and the golden fields of grain, the land drops dozens of feet to the rock-strewn shore and the churning blue sea. This was practice for the more distant, dangerous cliffs I'd discover in Ireland during my many trips to Cliffs of Moher and the Aran Islands.

I took my first steps at my great aunt and uncle's house on PEI and over decades of summertime visits, and countless long walks, I forged a deep and lasting connection with the land. In so many ways, the island was my muse. It still is. I would disappear for hours, my journal tucked under my arm, and I'd populate that rural corner of the world with an entire universe of stories. One year, probably just after I graduated from high school, I was writing about a realm where time stopped in the minutes before dawn. Though I'd been waking up in the dark to catch a school bus for ages, I realized I'd barely ever paused to watch the sunrise.

My family's home is tucked in the most picturesque fishing inlet you can imagine. A one-mile walk up the hill and then down a dirt lane that cuts across the fields will take you to cliffs that face north and east, overlooking the ocean waters in the Gulf of St. Lawrence. This was long before I had a cell phone that doubled as an alarm clock, so I have no idea how I woke in the dark. It's probably the same instinct that roused my mother. Only after I'd picked my way down the cliffs in the half-light to find a stone perch to watch the day begin did I realize she had followed me. I'd wanted to make this quest alone. Princess that I was, at the time I was annoyed that she spied on my sunrise. I can only pray I was kind on our walk home, but knowing the teenaged me, I was wrapped in the hoped-for solemnity of this mission and probably made it quite clear that I was irritated that she had encroached on my territory. Now, of course, I'm deeply grateful to know she cared to follow and I know I'll do the same to my daughters if given a chance.

The cliffs are the place to sit alone, contemplating the horizon. They're also the place to set a bonfire and share a bottle or two with some beloved companions. The cliffs are the place of freedom—of thought, of expression, of care. They are the place to celebrate the fantastic fragility of life with all of its potential for connection, as well as the potential for loss. They might be the place you contemplate Sovereignty for the first time.

Writing Prompt: The Cliffs and Your Map of Sovereignty

You've met my princess, and you've forgiven and celebrated your own princess. Pull out your Sovereignty Map again. Are there any landmarks that you need to add now that you've learned more about your princess energy and had a chance to remember your stories?

Remember that your Sovereignty Map helps you chart your dreams and your future, not just your memories and your past. If you never had a chance to explore your own actual or metaphorical cliff when you were younger, begin to imagine what they would look and feel like. Add it to your map and spend some time writing about a real or imagined journey to reach the territory of the princess.

CHAPTER 5

The Art of Claiming an Ancient Myth in Modern Times

So, I've mentioned the Sovereignty Goddess a dozen times or more, implying that you and she are already deeply devoted friends. That's probably not the case, is it? Though I've come to know her like a sister, a mother, a grandmother, I know she's not generally part of the conversation for people outside Celtic studies circles and the contemporary goddess movement.

For some, she is an earth goddess without a name, a great deity born before humans learned to pray to a white bearded guy on a throne in a gated community guarded by a saint named Peter. In some Irish stories, the Sovereignty Goddess is the land itself, and you can trace her hips and breasts in the mountain ranges. In other tales, she is a character who plays a role in the adventures of heroes and kings.

I cannot tell you when I first learned about her. It might have been at Boston College, the university I chose purely because of its extensive Irish Studies department. Then again, the Sovereignty Goddess might have reached for me in the witchy section of the women's bookstore I discovered not far from Harvard Square during my freshman year. Whether she was introduced by a tweed-wearing faculty member who taught me to find the juicy stories in obscure translations of medieval manuscripts or whether I found her in a "magic with a k" paperback about Neopaganism that urged me to believe I, too, could be a goddess, Sovereignty *spoke* to me. Her voice echoed through my uncommonly ordinary American childhood and back to other lifetimes when the Sovereignty and the goddess belonged to neither dusty study carrel nor new age circle. She spoke to me from the time and space where these stories were *real*.

The Sovereignty Goddess comes to us from across the Celtic world, but the tradition is strongest in countries I happen to love best: Ireland and Scotland. The land is experienced as inherently both sacred and feminine. If a goddess spoke to the dreams of a people, her story would eventually imprint the territory; countless mountains and other special places bear the name of ancient goddesses. Anyone who resonates with the idea of Gaia or Mother Earth instinctively understands this idea. We can feel it in our bones, even if we live in a city apartment or a sterile subdivision in the middle of America and have never known anyone who claimed to have a sacred relationship with a stretch of earth.

This divine being doesn't just show up in the contours of mountain ranges and rivers. When we do uncover stories in which the Sovereignty Goddess is a character with a pivotal role to play—and we tell a few in this book—there are some remarkable qualities that make her something other than just another divine being manipulating the fates of mortals. Three things generally happen when she appears on the scene: She proves herself to be a shapeshifter, she improves the fate of the land and its people, and she sleeps with a man in order to make him king. Otherworldly being that she is, the Sovereignty Goddess specializes in meddling in the affairs of men. And I do mean men. You don't tend to see a Sovereignty Goddess talking to a mortal sister, at least not in the oldest tales, but you do see her hopping in the sack with plenty of guys. It's unclear why this is the case, but we can probably blame the monks who wrote down the stories. Maybe they were just dudes perpetuating the longstanding belief that no one really cares about what happens in chick lit. As much as the Sovereignty Goddess is a force of nature fueled by her own supernatural powers, she is also a pawn in the games of earthly power brokers. The more things change over millennia, the more things stay the same, huh?

Let's get to know one of these Sovereignty Goddesses, the Lady Ragnell. She appears in the great body of legends about King Arthur and his kingdom of Camelot, which scholars place in fifth and sixth century Britain. Though Lady Ragnell's story has come to be associated with English writers—specifically the medieval writers Chaucer and Malory—the story is sourced from the same Celtic storytelling tradition that inspires Irish and Scottish stories. This story is everything and nothing like what we experience today, and that's exactly why it can teach us so much.

The Story of Lady Ragnell

Once upon a time, Arthur, the legendary king of Britain, was out hunting with his men. It was a fine day in spring, and he and his companions were glad to be free of the crowded castle where they'd spent the winter amidst the gossip and intrigue. This particular king loved his people and his land, but felt most himself when he was close to the earth. A man of his time—or maybe just a man—he most loved to get close to nature by killing things.

On the trail of a particularly fine specimen, Arthur crept quietly into a dense circle of trees. Sure of his aim, he loosed his arrow just as a dark form stepped into view. The sound of brush beneath the fleeing doe's hooves was explosive, but so was Arthur's sudden exclamation when he saw who had ruined his shot.

The Black Knight stood where the gentle animal had grazed a moment before. This hulking figure in his reeking dark furs with his thick dark beard hanging low over his chainmail tunic was the very opposite of innocent prey. Raising a great sword, the stranger bellowed, "You wronged me, man, when you stole away my lands and property and gave all to your nephew Gawain. And now, I will take my revenge!"

"Stop!" cried Arthur. Composing himself, the king remembered that he was Sovereign of this land and not just some defenseless creature—even if he had left his own blade on his saddle and he just loosed his last arrow. "You cannot kill your king, unarmed and unarmored as I am. That will bring no honor. Everywhere you walk, you will be shamed, a fallen knight who slayed a king in his most vulnerable moment."

The Black Knight appeared unmoved. Appealing to this scoundrel's sense of chivalry wasn't going to work. Arthur didn't get where he was by being a one-trick king, however. It was time to bargain. "What can I offer you—riches, a castle of your own? I will give you anything in my power to give. The whole of this land needs me. The peace of the lands depends on me. You must spare my life."

Arthur spoke true. From his castle in Camelot, Arthur ruled all of Britain during an era of unparalleled peace. A land scarred by invasion, infighting, and an endless quest to survive was united for a brief but beautiful time. But, of course, Arthur was human, and it appeared that he couldn't always keep track of his many knights and his many agreements.

"I want none of those. Nothing you could offer would replace what you took, that which was rightly mine!" the Black Knight boomed. "I care little for your land or its petty peace, but I will give you a chance to save your own life. One year from today, return to this wood without weapons, armor, or companions and answer to a riddle. Come back to me and tell me this: What is it that women desire above all else?"

The Black Knight melted back into the trees just as Arthur's band returned. Leading the group was Gawain, the very man who now was lord of the rogue knight's disputed land. Arthur told him what had happened and the young man instantly leapt into action.

"We will solve this mystery, my king! I shall ride in one direction and you in the other, and we shall ask every woman we meet to aid us with her answer. We will not permit that blackguard to triumph! You reclaimed those lands because the Black Knight would not steward them, would not tend to the fields or dispense justice to the people. He

will not be permitted to hold dominion over you. We shall uncover the answer!"

They set off. The king and his knight asked this question of every female they could find, presumably with open hearts and open minds. One woman said she desired fine gowns, another a full cauldron to feed her family, another to never be set aside by her husband. One woman wanted to ride astride a horse like a man, another simply wanted to ride her man. Another yearned for a child to fill her womb, another to be free of her husband so she could marry her own true love. The answers seemed as varied as the women who uttered them. Some were full of dreams, some of desperation. All these desires seemed too deeply personal to please a man such as the Black Knight. They had to give the villain credit—he had set his price on Arthur's life impossibly high.

As the twelfth month ended, they returned to Camelot, feeling further than ever from an answer that rang true.

Just before the castle gates, Arthur met a pockmarked old hag with rough patches of filthy gray hair. Her mouth was a busted, stinking maw that made a mockery of kisses. Her hands were gnarled talons that made a mockery of caresses. Her voice was a broken mill wheel, too low and too screeching all at once, that made a mockery of song. "Pass me by or stoop to speak to me, my king," she called out, "Either way, your life is in my hands."

Maybe Arthur stopped because it was his obligation as a monarch to his subject. Perhaps he was an honorable man who knew that helping old ladies was just something you had to do. Maybe he was feeling the desperation of an unsolved riddle and its deadly consequences. Either way, he stooped from his horse and fixed his attention on her.

"I know of your quest," she said, "I have the wisdom you seek, but to receive the answer that will save your life and this entire realm, you must grant my wish."

"Anything, lady," said Arthur. Though he would not climb from his horse to greet this old woman, he would treat her with respect. Especially if she had currency to offer such as this.

"Your most handsome and noble knight, Gawain... I will have him as my husband."

Arthur stared down at her, his own pretty, kissable mouth agape. Though his very spine twisted in revulsion, the fate of Britain, of Camelot, of his wife Guinevere, and the children she still hoped to bear, all hung in the balance. "I cannot force Gawain's hand, but I shall put the question to him, to see how he would answer in service to his king and his country. Tell me, woman, what is your name?"

"I am the Lady Ragnell," she said, with a rasp and belch. "And this is not a question, my king. It is a proposal." Arthur was already moving away, heavy with grief for his companion, yet hopeful for his nation. He moved at once with haste and with an aching slowness, knowing what his nephew's response would be.

Arthur was noble, but Gawain was something else entirely. He was more pure-hearted, faith-driven, loyal, and optimistic than all his companions put together. When the solemn king met his nephew in the great hall, the younger man quickly agreed. His only reply, "Is that all you ask of me? Of course, my king!"

The king felt it his duty as a friend to press the gravity of the issue and describe in detail the hideousness of the hag. "This is no lady you're agreeing to marry, my kinsman. This is a creature so foul as to barely be classed with the lowest washerwoman or the sourest old charwoman. I quake to think of how you will hate me when you see your fate."

Gawain brushed aside Arthur's warnings and again agreed, pledging his loyalty to the crown and to the lands they were sworn to protect. And so, Arthur returned to the gates. He ran this errand himself so that no one would know of this terrible bargain before it could be sealed. Too many maidens would swoon and too many of Gawain's fellow knights would object when they learned that such a punishment had been levied upon the greatest member of their company.

Arthur could smell the hag before he could see her. He did not look her in the eyes, one milky and sightless, one black and penetrating. He wished he could slam shut his ears when he heard her gleeful cackle when she learned she was to be a bride. His last hope—and his greatest fear—was that this so-called Lady Ragnell did not have an answer to the damnable riddle. "Before I marry you to my kinsman, the greatest of my company, I need to know the answer and I need to know it will please the Black Knight."

At the mention of the Black Knight she looked mightily displeased, but agreed to the bargain. Ragnell said, "Sovereignty. Sovereignty is what a woman wants above all else."

Sovereignty… That word was meant to be reserved for Arthur and those like him. It was meant for the well-born who inherited their thrones and for the warriors who had fought their way to the dais. As far as the king had ever seen or heard tell, that word was for men. But then, Arthur was a forward-thinking man (not to mention a desperate man), and he could see that the hag spoke true. What lay beneath the answers he'd received from farmers' wives, tanners' daughters, and the widows of the castle but the fundamental yearning for Sovereignty? With a nod of thanks, the king thundered back to the grove, for the year was nearly up.

The Black Knight awaited Arthur amongst the trees. Again, this hulking dark man was out of place in this delicate green place. The wide dark smile he wore was just as out of place in the midst of his wild beard. He was certain of his victory, certain that the king and his men would come back with some flimsy answer and then shower him with golden promises and stinking pleas for mercy. But Arthur wore his own smile, and it lit up his features like the sun upon a sweet meadow. A bit of a showman and confident that he held the key to his own freedom, Arthur told his adversary about the women he'd met. He described their longing for power and wealth, beauty and security, love and acceptance.

The knight was growing impatient at this little man's endless prattling and flexed his sword hand, ready to strike, but the king drew his story to a close just in time. "But then we found the truth..." said Arthur in a voice that echoed through the ring of trees. "Sovereignty. Women desire Sovereignty above all else."

The Black Knight howled. "You met that vile bitch of a sister of mine, didn't you? Ragnell told you, didn't she?" The king, now victorious, and quite confident that he was protected by the honor of a bargain well met, simply stared down his opponent. The villain quickly vanished from the scene, a one-man hurricane of fury who would blow his anger through other lands and plague other kings.

Arthur returned, one part victor and one part anguished friend. He told Gawain to prepare himself. Too weary of heart to face the woman who was his savior and his friend's tormentor, the king sent a pageboy to call the hag from the castle gates and usher her in through a side entrance.

Eventually, Arthur roused himself to meet her in the maze of underground storerooms. She was none too happy about being concealed in the cellars in this way, and when she heard Arthur's plans for an early morning wedding with only the birds of dawn to witness them, she roared as bitterly as the Black Knight. Indeed, it seemed the knight had spoken true and this old boot was in fact his sister. "Oh no," she exclaimed. "I shall have a proper wedding with a proper feast. All the court shall be in attendance to share Gawain's happy day. You owe me your life and this realm owes me everything... Sire." She spat that last word like a curse, and the king wondered if this new bargain would prove to be more bitter than any he could strike with the Black Knight. Again, with a heavy heart, Arthur went to his nephew and shared the lady's request. Still chivalrous, still eager (perhaps too eager, Arthur mused), Gawain agreed.

They were wed with full pomp and circumstance. The Lady Ragnell, all blemished and reeking, stooped in a most immaculate golden gown. The young Sir Gawain, all stalwart and loyal, wore a wan smile, but his respect was unwavering. Ripples of laughter moved through the crowd as they speculated about the night that stretched before the new couple. Gasps of horror were audible as they considered such youth wasted on such fearsome age.

When finally the court escorted them to their bedchamber and they were alone, Lady Ragnell turned to Sir Gawain, "And now it is time for you to show your true nobility, my husband. Kiss me quick as you would your true heart's bride."

And he did. Without signs of revulsion, without a trace of martyrdom, or a lick of young man's scorn for the old and unbeautiful, he kissed her. He didn't just offer her a regretful peck, but took her into his arms in a true embrace.

Maybe she had bewitched him. Maybe he saw something in her eye, something Sovereign, powerful, and good. The kiss lingered. He was not aware of her hairy upper lip, her crooked chin, her rotting teeth, her rough cheeks because, in his arms, his wife was transformed into a woman more fine than any he'd ever seen.

"Witchcraft!" he shouted, finally losing his noble demeanor.

She pulled him close again, "Not witchcraft," she said. "Marriage."

His chest heaving, his eyes wide, he staggered back from her. She smiled with a sweetness he'd never seen on this side of dreams. "You have broken the spell laid upon me by my wicked brother," she said. "He cursed me with ugliness because I would not give up my own sacred inheritance, my rich lands that stretch from the mountains to the sea. He had gambled away his own share and let the fields run fallow and the people wander leaderless. When he came to me he did not ask for charity, but demanded I give over all that was mine to rule and care for."

Gawain lifted her and swept his Lady Ragnell in a great circle, all full of joy and gratitude, proud of his own wisdom and even more proud to know he had married a woman of such beauty, wealth, and worth. The lady saw the joy in his face, and sighed as she knew she had to cast a shadow upon it. "A curse as dark as this, a curse from a heart as black as that of the Black Knight cannot be shed so easily, my beloved. I will always bear its taint. This beauty of mine has been

*restored, but only by half. It is your choice, my gentle husband...
Will you have me like this, all young and resplendent, by the light of
the day or by the glow of the moon?"*

*He looked at her, realizing that she was asking him if he would
share her glory with the court, and so be seen as a man of great
fortune, or if he would save her beauty for himself, and so be a man
with a bed blessed with passion. Still the same chivalrous creature in
relationship with his wife that he was with his king, Gawain replied,
"Oh, my lady, I could not possibly decide such a thing on your behalf.
It is your choice, my beloved, not mine."*

*And with that gift, the gift to choose her own way that had always
been her Sovereign birthright but had been so long denied, the spell
was broken utterly. Her beauty would glow both day and night. Her
power was brought back into balance, and wholeness was restored
not just for one woman or for one couple, but for the entire realm.*

How to Love a Myth, Flaws and All

Whoa. It barely seems possible that there's a story about one of
the greatest kings of legend spending a year trying to determine
what women want, but there it is. And look, their answer is *our*
answer. Thank the poets and the bards for preserving such a tale.
Unfortunately, it seems that everyone forgot about women's
desire entirely for several subsequent centuries. We only came
back to it again when the capitalists and their advertising teams
realized that satisfying women's needs could be quite profitable.
Though corporations have tried to tell us that women want a tiny
waist, big boobs, a huge diamond, and an easy way to get rid of
ring around the collar, we know the truth. The more women's
desires have changed over the millennia, the more they have

stayed the same. It's not about what you buy or even about whom you marry. Instead, it's about having the freedom and the safety to make choices, to feel safe, and to make the world a better place in your own way.

You might say that Ragnell reflects the experience of women across history. She has been abused. She has been cast aside. Her property has been stolen, and she has come to the hard realization that her worth is determined by her looks. It wasn't just her brother's cruelty that made her age a century in the space of a moment, but the entire patriarchal system of domination and oppression that made it impossible for her to securely rule her own lands and lead her own life. That said, she still retains her power and has the ability to affect the story. It's true that she needs to be recognized and chosen by men in order to change her circumstances and be "saved," but they need her, too. Arthur only holds onto the throne—and his head—because Ragnell offers him her wisdom. Without a woman to initiate him into a more complete version of manhood, Gawain is destined to follow his king around like an overeager puppy for the rest of his life. This woman and the men in her tale are in a reciprocal relationship, showing up to enact yet another scene in the perpetual masculine-feminine drama that has been at the heart of human consciousness from the very beginning.

A myth about a woman rescued and transformed by marriage can seem the very opposite of modern and empowering. And yet, even when we're feminists devoted to personal and creative Sovereignty, we still seek out relationship. There's a very good chance we harbor a private hope that being in relationship will solve some everyday problems from loneliness to the challenges that come with running a household alone. Myths have a way of reflecting our most troubling, complex needs back to us and inspiring us to undertake the quests we're most afraid to accept. As Karen Armstrong says in *A Short History of Myth*, "Myths are universal and timeless stories that reflect and shape our lives—they explore our desires, our fears, our longings, and provide narratives that remind us what it means to be human."[9]

The Sovereignty Goddess holds all of our archetypes in the arc of her story. She is the wise woman, the princess, and the queen all in one. She is the agent of the divine. She is the shapeshifter. She is kingmaker. This is all pretty neat, but does her story mirror ours enough to make it matter? We're flesh and blood mortals, and, chances are, we have no claim to royal blood. We've spent so much time feeling disempowered, it seems a bit mad to focus on a mythic character who exists to pass the monarchy onto someone else. Plus, no matter how magical our mindsets, we age according to the clock and no kiss is going to wipe away the wrinkles and those "stray eyebrows" that start sprouting from the chin. Our lives continue even after the love story reaches its climax, but these Sovereignty myths are light on the details of what "happily ever after" looks like for a hag turned hottie who has taken her spot in the royal bed. With the exception of Medb, the lusty warrior queen whom we met briefly at Rathcroghan and will get to know better a bit later on, the Sovereignty Goddess tends to melt into the background, presumably looking pretty and making royal babies, after the whole "I make you king" drama dies down. And then there's the ageism inherent in this tale. We seem to be perpetuating the obsession with youth and beauty when the heroine is "saved" from being the crone.

9 Karen Armstrong, *A Short History of Myth* (Edinburgh: Canongate, 2005).

The Sovereignty tales are an imperfect model, yes, but myth is unique in that it invites us to co-create with it, not just consume it. We are here to work with the plotlines, characters, and details that have been passed across the centuries and keep working them and growing with them so they become even more revelatory, relevant, and empowering. But still, what if people meet Sovereignty and just see another facet of the damsel in distress, the beleaguered helpmate, and the elder scorned? I'll be honest. There have been moments when I have worried that I'm trying to resuscitate themes and characters that should be allowed to fade into history, but I know that the transformative magic at the heart of these stories is mightier than their old sexist tropes.

From the outset, we established that this journey to Sovereignty is full of contradictions. We're weaving complex, phenomenal truths here, and sometimes it all seems more like a terrible maze than a meditative labyrinth. As the sex that gives birth and perpetuates the existence of the species, women possess a degree of awesome, absolute power. You'd think women would be worshipped and sanctified across the span of human history. Instead, the very opposite has been true. A woman has made every high king and every lowly peasant, but the most she could hope for in a patriarchal society was a kind husband, a roof over her head, a functional reproductive system, a good set of teeth, and a chance to be ignored by all the guys who wrote poems about epic battles.

The Sovereignty Goddess's continued relevance doesn't come from wielding power like the guys do—that story has been told too many times before. When we simply switch the boss's gender without changing the rest of the story, we just get a despot in a dress. Instead, the Sovereignty Goddess offers us her wisdom and her willingness to share her power with someone who is worthy of the job. Her power is in choice, not necessarily in rulership. Some of these Sovereignty stories *do* give us the choice to keep the crown and take the throne in a new way. However, as we'll learn in our exploration of the queen, the most satisfying power doesn't necessarily come from being at the helm. It comes from the fluidity, flexibility, and creativity that have long since been the purview of the feminine.

The magic we need right now is held in the twenty-first century feminist ideal that says "empowered women empower other women." That's why I took you into the Sovereignty Goddess's cave with me. I wanted you to witness the way the most incandescent being in the room proved her power by constantly bestowing her strength to others. This is why she is the perfect model for all of us who are caregivers, mothers, healers, and transformation agents dedicated to serving others' growth and change. She is a mistress of elevation, collaboration, and transformation. She knows how to take matters into her own hands and shift the direction of the tale. As students of her story who willingly fall under her spell, we're called to step into the cave and then reemerge to carry on the tradition.

In her time, Lady Ragnell was a Sovereignty Goddess because she served the land and its people. She helped the kingdom keep hold of a ruler who could offer collective peace and prosperity. Now, we see her as a Sovereignty Goddess because she's a herald for women's right to self-determination. We may appreciate the story for a different reason, but it's all the same energy. Instead of waiting around for a hero to save the day, we use our individual

Sovereign power of choice to better our own lives, and also create a world that offers peace and prosperity for all.

Writing Prompt: Hey There, Shapeshifter

Clearly, there is some serious sorcery at play as Lady Ragnell transforms from young maiden to hag and then back again. This isn't just a bit of fantasy fiction. All women are shapeshifters.

Sometimes, we become shapeshifters to accommodate others' needs and feelings. We may mute or transmute our personalities in order to fit the mood of a room.

Sometimes, we become shapeshifters because we're stepping into our power and stepping up our game. We find reserves of courage and strength to accomplish really big things.

Write about your own experience as shapeshifter. Be compassionate as you tell these stories and remember what you've learned from the princess. Practice forgiveness when you find instances when you betrayed your power and your truth. Celebrate when you realize that you rose to meet a challenge and stood in your Sovereignty.

CHAPTER 6

The Quest for Partnership and the Question of Romantic Love

All of the Sovereignty myths in this book are a mix of sex and power, romance and rulership. That's true of just about every great story that captures the imagination. Chances are, your favorite dramas include panoramas of the battlefield interspersed with stolen kisses and meaningful glances. My own dreams are a blend of romantic interludes and the adventures of the independent warrior. I long to be both passionate partner and lone wolf. I admit that I'm still the girl who feels she's supposed to be made of sugar and spice and dreams that love affairs are nice. And, at the very same time, I hold tight to a belief in a woman's right to be as feisty, freewheeling, and autonomous as she wants to be. Both. I always want *both*.

"Both" is a good thing. Both is an essential thing. We get into philosophical and practical trouble when we buy into what they call "the myth of separation" and start to bind ourselves with either/or boundaries. This is where the division between sacred and profane, feminine and masculine, good and bad comes in. This is the stuff of conservative fundamentalist preachers and divisive politics. It's the "us and them" worldview of racial segregationists and high schools that can't deal with gender-neutral bathrooms. And when we buy into the belief that we can either be Sovereign or be in love, we're playing a version of the same nasty game. I hate that game.

I stand up for my right to choose. I stand Sovereign in my own body and in my own sense of self. I stand Sovereign within my partnership. (Most of the time—and when I don't, I try to look hard at what is mine to change and whether it's still possible to hold onto my sense of Sovereignty within the relationship.) No matter what happens, I stand Sovereign in my right to choose *both*. Both the bedroom and the office. Both motherhood and work. Both him and me. Both my Sovereignty and my marriage.

My experience of Sovereignty is happening inside a relationship right now, but that's certainly not the only way. Many of the writers and coaches who talk about these ideas of self-reliance and autonomy reached the concept on the other side of divorce. I bless all women who find themselves outside of a partnership for one reason or another and joyfully acknowledge that we are more alike than we are different. In the story I am living (at least for right now), Sovereignty issued her invitation in the midst of monogamous married life and I'm called to hone my practice of *both*.

Sovereignty has tested me and my commitment to myself, to him, to us. Sovereignty constantly asks me if I can truly access princess, queen, and wise woman within me—even if I'm not free to explore the cliffs on my own, even if I have to share a castle, even if I can't just disappear to my own cave and live by my own rules. Sovereignty has asked me if I can be a true shapeshifter within a relationship that demands consistency. She asks if I can stay true to myself even when this union and this family we've built require most things to stay the same. Again and again, I've said, "Yes, thank you. At the moment, I don't need to shed my skin or make every decision independently in order to be fully myself in the midst of this marriage." Even if it's hard. Even if it's counterintuitive. Even if it takes communication, diplomacy, and certain forms of compromise. Even if partnership seems the least direct route to Sovereignty, such is the nature of this knotted-up life I get to live. Such is the nature of this gloriously complicated life I continue to choose each day.

But I don't want to candy coat these choices and make it sound as if simply declaring "I'm Sovereign!" will make marriage, divorce, or the single life any easier. Instead, we're relational beings who are called to seek and grow our Sovereign selves inside relationship. Sometimes, we find ourselves hitched to people who are hell-bent on making it all impossible. The only Sovereign solution might be to get the hell out of there, but that's rarely easy or comfortable. Especially when you're a mother.

(Extra)Ordinary Sovereignty

On a gorgeous spring morning not long ago, the trees wore bright green baubles instead of leaves and the dogwoods spoke to the cherry trees about how fine the magnolias were looking. This sweet weather story was in vivid contrast to the stories of pain that glowed from my screen.

Three social media posts. Three brave and brilliant mothers whose lives had been torn apart by relationships that, once upon a time, were supposed to be based on love. They'd fought, and were still fighting, for their children. They'd fought, and were still fighting, for their own liberty. One woman was celebrating a milestone moment in her marriage, though she'd been free of that union for a dozen years. Her younger child was turning eighteen and she was finally able to cut the final cord now that she no longer had to endure joint custody with an abusive ex. Another woman was just starting the legal battle with her former spouse because her younger daughter was threatening self-harm if she had to spend one more weekend with her father. And one woman wasn't able to post about her struggles on Facebook because she's in the county jail awaiting sentencing after a murder conviction. She shot the devil in the house, the boyfriend who had been brutalizing her for years, because she was terrified he'd kill himself and her after child services had been called in to check on their young kids.

In every case, there was abuse—physical, emotional, all of the above. In every case, the system that is supposed to protect people and families showed itself to be an inhuman machine that was on the side of money and power. Women's and children's lives had been ripped apart and continued to be ripped apart, terribly ever after. In every case, these women are warriors of Sovereignty. They had the courage to end the relationship, even though they were terrified. They continue to draw on seemingly limitless reserves of courage to keep fighting for their rights and their freedom, and for the happiness and safety of their babies. In every case, I know these women well: a beloved community member, a cherished colleague, a loving mom at the preschool.

The stories of women enduring hellacious marriages, going through vicious custody battles that get reignited with every weekend exchange, sitting in a courtroom being told by a jury that it was murder, not self-defense... These are not just "stories." They are not statistics from NPR or women's studies classes. These are the truths of women's lives. This is when the quest for Sovereignty steps out of the pages of old books and becomes real. These women, and countless women who have decided that their children's safety, their own self-worth, and their own survival is worth the risk of getting out and being alone: They are my living sheroes. The women who never chose to be alone but find themselves to be single parents are, too. That spring morning trip into social media also included brave words from a dear friend, a new widow, who is trying to find her way through life as a mama to three without the man she still loves. I weep for her and for every woman who has lost her partner to illness, to accident, or to suicide.

Compared to these survivors, these mama bears and warrior goddesses, my battles have been the stuff of toy soldiers and paper dolls. They've faced the demons, made their own ultimate courageous decisions, stood up, and walked away. And they've still kept on fighting because it's never really over when you're a mom. These women teach me about what Sovereignty looks like, what motherhood looks like: a lifelong commitment, if not a lifelong struggle.

These women and their stories teach us that judgment has no place here. Yes, in some lives, the quest for Sovereignty is a brutal and bloody one, fought in the courts and with your own hands. For others, the movement toward Sovereignty is more subtle; the pain and struggles seem less dramatic, at least on the surface. We are called to learn from one another, to share our experiences, to share healing and share the burden when appropriate. We are called to recognize all the binds that imprison our sisters, to validate what women do to get free of them, and to share the wisdom that got us through. Sometimes it's a traumatic event that catapults us into the center of the Sovereignty Map, exploring unknown territory in the quest for agency and trust in our own worth. Sometimes it's a low-grade nagging need that forces us to really start searching for our own crown.

Love, War, and Eighties Movies

Want to know why I am so fascinated by shapeshifting goddesses and spend so much time imagining how they speak to the truth of modern women's lives?

Sovereignty doesn't come naturally to me. Partnership does.

This became a puzzle that my equal parts romance-driven and feminist-fueled heart just needed to figure out. Because I am built to be in relationship to another person—be it the man I love, a business collaborator, or a best friend—I felt driven to study and embody Sovereignty in a conscious, deliberate way. After all, there's no place you need Sovereignty more than in the beautiful and terrible tangle of relationship.

There's that feminist slogan from the sixties: *a woman needs a man like a fish needs a bicycle.* This iconic phrase was pinned to my dorm room wall, but it was more aspirational than anything else. Truth is, I've always been here for the love story. Most people see *Star Wars* as the ultimate hero's journey, an intergalactic battle between good and evil. Me? It's always been about the kissing. When I was four years old, I christened myself Princess Leia and the other preschool moms would have to invite "Leia" over to play because no one knew my real name. I wanted to be Princess Leia because she was pretty, royal, and had a hell of a lot of moxie. I also wanted to be her because I thought her boyfriend was dead sexy (though I wouldn't have phrased it quite like that in 1983). The princess declared her love and the scoundrel of a hero responded, "I know." Yet another generation was being indoctrinated into a lopsided, half-baked courtship narrative and taught to believe they were witnessing another epic, enviable romance. To that, I still say, "Pass the popcorn." And only when I'm done being entertained will I realize I've fallen for the same old enchantments that have held me in their fantastical, superficial thrall from the very start.

These days, we make internet memes to celebrate that our princesses all became generals. Carrie Fisher would become General Organa and Robin Wright would evolve from being Buttercup in *The Princess Bride* into the quintessential warrior woman, General Antiope in *Wonder Woman*. Proudly, I buy tickets to this cultural evolution of girl power, but part of me is still looking over my shoulder. I long for the days when there was no reason to second-guess my soul-deep desire to fall rapturously in love. Then and now, I'd rather make out than wage war, and I'm not totally sure I am psyched that the alternative to being a princess is wielding a sword or commanding the Rebel Alliance in the face of near-certain doom. It's easy to cheer for these renegade rulers with an Instagram post, but it's a hell of a lot harder to embody this energy in your own life. Especially when your actual life is built around marriage and child-rearing and co-signing a mortgage, rather than taking out the Empire and defending the island of the Amazons.

When you turn off the TV, tune into the desires that have shaped you, and realize you have a heart preprogrammed for romantic love, you just might realize you'd rather deal with the snoring and the whiskey-scented breath than sleep alone. The question then becomes: "What do I really desire?"

I realized that I was a princess back when I started reckoning with how much I depended on my husband and my dad for financial and emotional support. It took much longer to fully inhabit my queen self. A key moment in that process came the night I finally recognized my marriage could not and should not sit at the center of my life. It happened the night I realized that not only did my marriage not satisfy all of my desires, but that in trying to make it do so I was yearning for something I didn't even really want and didn't even fully believe in.

But before we get to the moment of marital death and rebirth, let me introduce you to the other character in this story. In so many ways, I am married to the wonderful, typical "American white guy." He works himself beyond exhaustion for a company that's great in some ways and laughably horrible in many others. He says he doesn't do feelings, and often deflects serious conversations like a dude in an Adam Sandler movie, but he's got a soft streak seventeen miles wide. He is fiercely loyal and dedicated to his family. Sometimes, though, he still tells me that he wonders how he woke up in this life, a husband and a dad. If I was programmed for romantic love and the whole wedding-house-kids progression, he was programmed to work hard, numb out, and take a wait-and-see approach on the whole settling down thing.

Though part of me longed for a soul mate who would read me poetry and take me to the theater and have the kind of abs that make a smart woman do silly things, I'd had that in other relationships and things had still gone down in flames. When it all comes down to it, the chemistry was there—and still is. If Han Solo's "I know" was good enough for Leia, it was good enough for me. Plus, Han would eventually say "I love you" in *Return of the Jedi* and my husband has always been quite free with those three little words. Considering I had been taught to ask for little more than a good-hearted, emotionally unavailable man who was doomed to burn with largely inexpressible passions, I was ahead of the game in many ways. Even if a cage of modern masculinity built of overwork, college football, and microbrews tries to hide it, there's great passion, emotion, and presence in this man of mine.

He respects my body and my moods and understands I need to hide in a red tent of my own making one day per month. We laugh together and lose ourselves in the same epic movies and TV shows. And he cleans the house. It's more than that, though. There's the way we complete one another's sentences—even if we often differ on so many of the things that "should" matter from spirituality to intellectual interests to social issues. As we realized from the beginning, he is the earth and I am the air, and humans need a balance of both to survive. After all these years, I know ours to be a soul contract.

After all these years, I also know that soul contracts do not need to mean we need to stay in relationship forever. But I have stayed. On some level, it's for the sake of the kids, for the sake of our shared material world, for the sake of my identity as a married woman. To varying degrees, all of those things are real and all of those things matter. In my darkest moments, I would admit I've stayed because there's nothing worse than the thought of his face on the other side of the negotiating table. To think of him, staring at me over a wall of betrayal, all the love he had for me gone… I cringe at the thought.

As I've interrogated my marriage and tried to figure out how far we're meant to go together, how much of my Sovereign territory he's meant to have access to, I have asked if I really do stay for convenience, fear, or pride. A willingness to examine your choices and habits is an essential part of Sovereignty. You need to be willing to walk to the edge of the comfortable world, the safe world, the shared world, and look into the void beyond. Remember, the cliff is the realm of the princess. Funny, she is the one who got me into this mess with her mangled perspective on love and romance, but she also plays a key role in helping me navigate the aftermath of tying the knot, of deciding when to strengthen it and when to sit down to the work of untangling things.

The princess within me is brave enough to take me out to where the land meets the sky. She holds my hand and we look down and we wonder about taking the jump back into the single life. It's only the princess in me who knows what it means to be uncoupled, after all. She'll remind me how she survived it, all the books she read and all the unencumbered fun she had. She'll remind me of how lonely and scared she was, too. We'll cry and laugh and sing Ani DiFranco and Sinead O'Connor songs about not being a pretty girl and about being no man's woman. We'll imagine what a forty-year-old me might be like without a man to hold me tight and to hold me back.

But then, when the bonfire we've lit at the end of my known world begins to burn down, and the flask of whatever it is we've been passing back and forth runs dry, my princess will look at me and remind me that I am wired for love and partnership. She will remind me that I undoubtedly could thrive on my own, but that I don't need to be an unmarried woman to meet her at the cliff from time to time. I don't have to choose between my wildest inner child and the committed queen. And she reminds me of something essential, something I tend to lose track of when I make my husband into a caricature and I see my own life as a two-dimensional, either/or world that's built on the bare and ugly question of "Should I stay or should I go now?" He's not asking me to choose between myself and him. He loves the spark and the sparkle in me. He always has. There's still a shared spark that guides me back to our shared castle, to our shared bed.

And then I can gather the strength to really look at the soul-deep cringe that comes on when I imagine saying goodbye to him in a lawyer's office: I cringe not because I fear his anger but because I love him.

We share enough. And what we don't share… That's where the light of Sovereignty gets in.

A Single Night

When I met this guy I'd later marry, I was a wannabe Sovereignty Goddess armed for a knife fight. Fresh out of a relationship that failed because I hadn't yet succeeded at loving myself, I was going to slice to ribbons anyone who tried to get between me and my independence.

My adult life to that point had been a story of having, or not having, a relationship. I'd spent most of high school wishing for a boyfriend, fell into the closest thing I'd ever have to a fairytale romance, and then lost the first half of college racking up long-distance charges. Eventually aching for freedom as much as I'd ached for love, I broke it off just before my junior year abroad. Then I stumbled through the second half of my college years searching for a hookup. Though I was passionate about my women's studies classes, the fierce feminist ideals of authors like bell hooks and Mary Daly became illegible as soon as the sun went down. After a few beers, I became an insecure co-ed motivated by that arcane desire to be chosen by an eligible young man (translation: any drunk guy who seemed vaguely nice and interested in sticking his tongue down my throat). Shortly after I landed in Dublin for grad school, I picked up another long-distance relationship with someone I'd dated briefly in Boston. We stayed together for a couple years after I returned to the States, but our relationship faded away shortly before my twenty-fifth birthday, so I moved out of our shared apartment to live on my own in a small college town.

Though I was dying to reclaim the decade I'd lost to boy trouble, old habits die hard. On my first Friday night alone in that tiny new place that boasted neither cable nor internet, I decided I couldn't just stay home alone with my new kitten. And so I did "brave" the only way I knew how. I stowed my journal in the shoulder bag I'd picked up at the army surplus store (this was 2004 and this may actually have been fashionable, or at least the right kind of avant-garde) and I headed into the village. Tea in a paper cup while writing mediocre lonely-girl poetry seemed like my best bet, but at the last moment, I thought better of it. Any American woman could spend a solitary evening in a Starbucks, but I reminded myself I'd lived in Ireland and I could take myself out to a bar.

I put myself in the crowded saloon where my future husband and his friends were throwing back yet another round. He'd be the first and last stranger to ever pick me out of a crowd and ask the bartender what the girl at the end of the bar was having. I told him straight out that he would have to accommodate himself to my new confident, carefree, single-woman lifestyle. Correction: I drank a few more beers, kissed him, took him home, and took the morning-after pill, and *then* I told him he'd have to tuck himself into my "busy learning how to be Sovereign on my terms" schedule. Nightly yoga classes and nurturing friendships with women would come before you, I told him. And still, this guy had it *bad*. He'd slip into my apartment and have dinner ready for me when I got home from an evening out. This all suited us both just fine. It turns out that I like the idea of staying fiercely independent while being held in the safety of a relationship. He liked being the port I came home to.

As it turns out, independence tends to erode in captivity. I got pulled into the center of our relationship's heaviness. By the time we were married, I went to yoga rarely and only had a small social circle in our town. Nightly drinks on the couch just became cozier and easier. Once kids were part of the picture, Netflix after bedtime was our only shared oasis. Wasn't this what love looked like after the princess and her hero fell in love and saved the world? Well, maybe. But it's easy to see why the storytellers conclude with the deep passionate kiss that marks the end as well as the beginning. It's not really worth writing an epilogue if it's essentially just going to say "they were generally happy enough and endured the responsibilities of settled adulthood ever after."

We may call on princesses and queens—characters out of fantasy—to help us understand our quest for Sovereignty, but this has always been a quest to fully inhabit reality. And for that, we need healthy, heaping doses of wisdom.

Dark Moon Love

One dark night, years after the vows were said and the babies born, I stood alone, pressing my face against the bathroom window, looking up and hoping for the impossible. There was nothing to see, but I longed to find some measure of comfort in the light I knew I wouldn't find. I sought confirmation in the shadow. Somewhere I'd read that this particular new moon in Gemini was all about yearning and recognizing our own lack of influence over the earth. I needed to think about what kind of influence I actually had over my own life. My ideas about Sovereignty told me that I had quite a lot, but then why did I feel so powerless? Some astrologer's blog said, "This is the time to bring ourselves into alignment with the deeper current of sacred becoming in our own life." It was grammatically unwieldy, and, like all generalized astrology it only made sense if you needed and wanted it to. This was a night when I needed things to make sense for me. The words were failing me, so I just squinted up to the clear, dark skies and looked for my reflection in the absent moon.

My husband and I were recovering from the worst argument we'd had in recent memory, and for once, I hadn't seen it coming. To me, this had been a typical stretch of family life. Everyone was busy and tired, but this was what we'd signed up for and we were making it work. That wasn't his experience. Under his "stressed, exhausted, but such a good sport" exterior, things were feeling dark. It was his stuff. It was our stuff. It was the accumulated stuff that comes with aging parents, demanding employers, marvelously relentless children, the vagaries of marriage, unresolved pain, and the sense of isolation that comes with trying to be all things to all people.

I believe we could have lost one another that particular night, but in the midst of the conflict, I chose the version of the story where we stayed together. Just as I trust in my own Sovereignty, I trust the Sovereignty of others. It's not my job to handle pest control when I meet the demons that inhabit my spouse's soul. Except when it is. Occasionally, being in a partnership means stepping into warriorship and lifting the sword that's grown too heavy in the hands of my beloved. That night, it was my job to beat back the monsters and protect the marriage. That night, when things got ugly, I didn't dissolve into tears and launch into every supercharged emotion under the sun. For once, I didn't take things personally. I was able to respond to his words rather than explode with fear and reactivity. I believe that approach saved us. Don't get me wrong, he was out of line for projecting his unprocessed angst on me. And to be clear, there was a lot going on between us that I hadn't wanted to see, things that I did need to step up and take responsibility for. I never want to repeat that experience, but I am more proud of that night than any other night we've spent together.

This was a moment that could have broken us and it didn't. My hold on Sovereignty meant I could hold the sword to defend us both. I could hold the *us* in the proper context and remember that I had energy to spare to hold onto *me.*

As we recovered over the following days and nights, I needed to keep holding myself, safe and Sovereign. At this point, however, I was also tired and lonely and wanted a warm place to land as I took stock of how close we'd come to ending it all. I wanted him near me even as I wrangled with the realization that he couldn't make it all better. Sovereignty and self-reliance were grand, but on this particular new moon night, I wanted my husband to turn off the damn hockey game—even if it was game seven—and put repairing our relationship and a good long hug above spectator sports and another work deadline. And yet, as much as I hated to acknowledge it as I gazed at the moonless sky through a glaze of tears, I realized I was getting exactly what I needed. Alone with myself and the pages of a brand-new journal and a great black sky, I entered the undiscovered territory where I could fall into that sacred becoming that the astrologer said was flowing in with the lunar tide.

I needed to shift my own center of gravity. Permanently.

Sitting in the middle of a big empty bed, I opened to a fresh page in my journal and scrawled "Our marriage is not the most important thing in our lives." Something felt different—and a little bit tragic—when I saw this on the page. In this case, I wasn't casting a spell. I was simply admitting a truth that was even truer than my desire for romantic love. Breathing deep, I was sorting through my realities and my fantasies when it came to commitment, passion, and the ingredients of happiness. The princess came forward to claim my dashed dreams. She carried them back to her cliffs because I no longer had need of them. I wasn't abandoning every romantic ideal, but I was done with them for a while. I was meant to be Sovereign in my own life and capable of crowning myself queen, after all. I was meant to sit and sip the cup of my own presence and potential. It was time to quit hoping that one great kiss or a dramatic gesture would fill me and fuel me and make it all okay. I was meant to be in partnership, but I was also meant to be free.

Even though I longed to know I came before my husband's distraction, duty, and pain, coming first wasn't essential to my happiness. In fact, it wasn't even essential to the long-term success of our marriage.

In more than ten years together, I thought I had to build my life around our relationship and placed the "us" at the center of my life. I'd been trying to find my story inside a myth of Us that was never meant to carry me or him all the way through. This didn't mean our marriage meant any less now. It simply meant that I was finally learning that no amount of dedication to romantic love and the ideal of couplehood was ever going to save us. But being Sovereign in my own soul and my own skin? That just might get everyone their happy ending.

Sovereignty is never about avoidance and isolation—even though telling everyone to fuck off might feel like the most simple and satisfying choice. Sometimes, you hurt so badly from a hundred different things, you feel ready to burn down the barn and blow up your whole life, just to see the moon. Sometimes, you get so busy looking down at all the earthly catastrophes, you don't realize that the moon isn't even in the sky. Destroying the life you share with one other chosen person won't necessarily make the sky any brighter. Life doesn't get any easier just because you've decided you don't need anyone and no one needs you.

As much as I believe that the wisdom of astrology can help us understand the human experience and that there's a sacredness to the cycles of the heavens, the actual light of the moon doesn't matter. It's all about the light within and whether we can move away all the clouds and the bullshit and use it to guide the way.

That tremendous argument and its lonely, life-shifting aftermath happened a couple of years ago now. Sometimes I slip and revert to living like there was a "we" rather than a "me" at my core. I look to him to make me feel good about myself, our marriage, and the world, and I'm always let down. It's not his job and it's not something the Sovereign being in me can expect. I have a marriage that is messy and human, that is full of love and conflict, and that is still worth holding onto. It's a hard, cruel world and too many women have monsters in their beds. I am grateful that I have a kind, powerful, yet fallible man beside me and, at least for now, my path to Sovereignty is best traced with him. This partnership is meant to continue for as long as it makes us stronger—as individuals, as parents, as people who deserve to love and be loved. If it begins to feel like all that knots us together is a cruel bind rather than a strong, secure one, then we'll consider a change.

I'll ditch the poetry and speak to the practical: It is possible to stand Sovereign while within a committed partnership. Being married to someone who can help cover your basic needs can be essential to experiencing your creative and spiritual Sovereignty. Sometimes this sounds less appealing than proclaiming yourself wild, sexy, Sovereign, and free, but it can work. It can do more than simply "work." Love and commitment, Sovereignty and agency, independence and interdependence are not mutually exclusive.

To the women who have found the courage to leave an abusive relationship, I say, "You are a goddess." To those who are still there, I say, "I understand and I send you strength to survive the day and to rewrite the future." To those who left an unfulfilling marriage because you knew there's more to life than what you can experience in the confines of your coupleship, I say, "More power to you." To those who've found a partner with whom you can be completely and unapologetically yourself, I say, "Hallelujah! Enjoy it!" To those who are single and without children, I admit I'm a little envious and I celebrate that research shows you're counted in the happiest demographic and will outlive us all. And for those, like me, who are riding through the rough patches, getting lost and then getting found, and over time continuing to find a reason to say, "Yes, let's go for a spin around the sun for another year, beloved," I see you.

Sovereignty is at once a shared journey and a singular journey, regardless of whether you file a joint tax return or not. No matter what your relationship status, you have an unalienable right to

Sovereignty and any partnership that's worth sustaining will make that possible.

Writing Prompt: Your Love Stories

Not every love story belongs in a romance novel. Instead, your real stories are probably more surprising, painful, wild, sweet, and impossible.

Have you lost yourself in a love story? Write into what it felt like to surrender your Sovereignty to gain love. It might have been with a romantic partner, but it could be with a friend or another family member.

Have you found yourself when you found someone to love? Tell a story of claiming your Sovereignty and strengthening your relationship in the process.

CHAPTER 7

Crown the Queen

I will make incursions
through the fertile land of Ireland
my battalions all in arms
my amazons beside me
(not just to steal a bull
not over beasts this battle—
but for an honour-price
a thousand times more precious—
my dignity).
I will make fierce incursions.

—From *"Medb Speaks"* by Nuala Ní Dhomhnaill,
translated from the Irish by Michael Hartnett[10]

10 Nuala Ní Dhomhnaill, *Selected Poems: Rogha Dánta* (Dublin: New
Island Books, 2000).

When I started learning about living in Sovereignty, I just wanted to get free of that frail and foolish thing, the princess. I hadn't even started to think about how the wise woman figured into it all. Instead, I wanted to nab the crown that would show everyone I had the wealth, the status, and the wherewithal necessary to survive this brutal, grown-up world. Once I wore that kind of hardware, I assumed I would be untouchable. It was all about the day when I could be the bold boss lady who could show everyone I was all kinds of secure, intentional, and capable.

But of course, life had already showed me that I might check one box after another—marriage, motherhood, motherlessness—but no one was going to book the hall for my coronation or plan a parade to mark the beginning of my reign. Clearly, becoming queen of my own life was nobody else's business but mine. There would be no single point of arrival. There would be no clean narrative. Becoming queen wouldn't be instantaneous, easy, or even all that desirable much of the time. Eventually, I would come to realize that it's never been about "becoming" the queen in the sense of unlocking a new level of achievement, as if we lived in an eighties Nintendo game. My way of being queen wouldn't rely on taking over, making millions, or showing the world I was one tough broad. At this point, I understand that being queen is more about being a smart, benevolent manager than it is about accepting accolades and adoration from a crowd that just loves the royals. It's definitely more about offering care and concern than it is about being viewed as a distant, invincible monarch. The queen within helps me inhabit a certain "I've got this" energy in a consistent, conscious way when it's necessary—and then I give her as much time off as I possibly can.

There's something remarkable about the way Sovereignty is personified in Celtic myth: For all that she is the embodiment of power, land, and rulership, the Sovereignty Goddess is rarely the woman in command of the realm. Someone like Lady Ragnell has that power, loses it, and shares her land with her husband in the end. At first, I thought this was a problem with the whole Sovereignty model. It seemed like we would have to redouble our efforts in order to place women on the throne. The deeper I go, however, the more I realize that this concept of queen is confounding and complicated and almost as likely to be marked by what we *don't* want to be than by what we do.

The crowns we wear are shaped by who we are and what we choose, but they're also shaped by the world and its demands. Yes, we can stand Sovereign, choosing how we respond to situations and choosing the people we associate with, but there's a hell of a lot we cannot control. Genetics, the color of our skin, the health and wealth of our parents, brain chemistry, the state of the global economy, the quality of the air, and the communal access to water are just the easiest to name.

Queenship isn't permanent or immutable. Like every other role we inhabit as we cycle through the Sovereignty Knot, queenship is meant to be transitory. If you think you're signing up for a "dictator (compassionate or otherwise) for life" arrangement, you're going to be disappointed. And deposed. Life itself will steal your crown, but your own princess and wise woman will also be there to help pluck it from your head. There's simply more to life than being in charge. The more I come to understand about Sovereignty, the more I realize that the queen is most powerful when she's *not* obsessing over the throne.

You met Medb briefly on the other side of that wild ride to Rathcroghan, the royal seat from which she ruled her own vast Irish province. Let me tell you more of her story and then we'll walk through all these conflicting ideas about the potential—and the pitfalls—of wearing the crown. Medb was built for conquest and secured her right to rule in the battlefield by whatever means necessary. She'll also add an interesting layer to all this talk of monogamous marriage, too. Medb, too, was built for partnership, but she interprets that in a very different way than I do.

The Story of Medb

Fadó fadó…

A woman and her husband lay in bed after the rest of the royal household was asleep. King Ailill rolled over, ready for a bit of pillow talk. "You've done well, haven't you, my queen?"

Queen Medb smiled, "Yes, husband. It's been a long, rich life."

Ailill got a strange look in his eye, "Of course. But particularly since we were wed."

She arched a brow, "I've got a good, steady man to share my bed, if that is what you mean. Not that I was lacking in lovers before, of course, but to rule beside a king such as you, an equal in every way, that truly is something."

Maybe it's just because this was necessary to move the story forward. Maybe it was because Ailill wasn't really a match for Medb— though she thought he had every quality on her non-negotiable list, being generous, brave, and without jealousy or fear. Or maybe it was because he was the perfect match for her. Whatever the reason, Ailill pressed the issue. "Well, of course," he said. "But I wouldn't count those womanly assets you took to our union as equal to what I brought."

Medb sat up in bed, and turned on her husband, "What are you talking about, boyo?" She went on to list the men at arms, the vast lands, and the fat herds she had brought to their marriage. She reminded Ailill that she was the daughter of the High King of Ireland and that she was gifted her own province and that all of Connacht would rise when she lifted her hand.

He reminded her that he, too, was a king's son. "My elder brothers each were awarded their kingdoms, so I came in search of you, the only queen in Ireland with your own lands. With my pedigree—and my wealth—who was a better mate for you, the daughter of the king of all Ireland, than I?"

Medb leapt up, and she may well have stomped her foot, too. "You've got a lot of nerve, mister, insinuating that I needed you. I, a Sovereign in my own right. I, a woman who has never had one man without another standing in his shadow. I, a woman who will take a moonblood piss in a field before a battle and create such a gulch as you'd see it there in the landscape for a few thousand years. You are the one who moved up in the world, not the other way around, darling."

Don't let the raised voices fool you. These two were well matched. Ailill rose to meet her and captured her in a kiss. Passionate tempers subsided into passionate love making, but the debate raged even after their bodies were sated. They awoke every single member of the household to help with the accounting of their worldly goods and vassals. By the next dawn they had gathered every soldier, every bit of gold and bronze, every bolt of cloth, every mare, sow, ewe, and heifer—and all their mates and offspring, too.

The rows of belongings and assets were equal, down to the last pot and jug.

Save one.

A white bull had been born in Medb's herd, but he refused to be mastered by a woman, so he moved over to join Ailill's cattle. This was the deciding factor. Medb was furious. Ailill tried to hide his grin.

Having seen similar tempests before, Mac Roth, Medb's most faithful messenger, whispered in her ear. "I have seen a brown bull that's finer, my lady. He goes by the name Donn Cuailnge and he lives in the house of Daire Mac Fiachna in Ulster."

The queen grinned, "Excellent! Go to him and ask that I may have the loan of the bull for one year and a day. Offer him fifty heifers as payment. If he should accompany you, promise him a tract of land that would stretch from my throne to the sea. You can also offer him the friendship of my own thighs."

And so Mac Roth was accompanied by a delegation of eight men. They went and put the offer before the chieftain in Ulster, who heartily agreed to deliver the bull and take up Medb's friendly bonus offer, too.

Everyone in Daire's court celebrated with a toast. And then another. And another. And another. When Medb's messengers finally got to bed, they'd lost any trace of tact or sense they'd been born with. One confided in the other, "Ah well, 'tis nice the old man agreed. Our Medb would have forced him to give that bull over in one quick and mighty raid!" As the two laughed, the head of the chieftain's household entered through a side door. He asked them to repeat their boasting and, no smarter than any pair of drunkards usually were, they did.

When the messengers awoke the next morning, their sore heads were made worse by the news that neither the bull nor his master were coming with them. They returned to their queen and her king empty-handed.

Medb shook her head, understanding just how the situation had gone down. She sighed. "Why am I not surprised?" Though she didn't say aloud, you could feel the unspoken phrase typical men *hanging in the air.*

"Well, my beloved Medb," said Ailill, "Your name does mean 'she who intoxicates,' does it not?"

She looked at her husband with a wry expression. "Indeed," she muttered. Let's imagine she drank deep from the goblet at her elbow and said in a voice that echoed through the feasting hall, "Are we up for a battle, then?" In full warrior's regalia, Medb led the charge to Ulster in an open chariot. Her husband was on one side, her favorite lover Fergus on the other.

The rest of the story is a complicated one full of battle, blood, destruction, curses levied, and prophecies upheld. Medb would have her advantages in this battle—a sister Sovereignty Goddess Macha had doomed the men of Ulster to fall with the pains of a woman in childbirth in their most desperate hour. It would have been an easy victory for the raiders of Connacht if not for one great Ulster warrior who was immune to such curses. Cúchulainn's stories belong in another book, but for the purposes of this one, know that he may have fought off the invading armies, but Medb eventually manage to steal the bull herself.

When they all got back home to the west, the great White Bull who had once deserted Medb's herd for Ailill's fought against the great Brown Bull of Ulster. The two animals killed one another, and Medb's and Ailill's fortunes were, at last, equal.

They did suffer a great mutual loss, however. At various points during the battle, the contentious couple had offered their daughter Finnabair to several different warriors in hopes of making alliances that would strengthen their side. Eventually, it's revealed that the princess has been promised to seven different kings at once. When seven hundred men were slaughtered in the subsequent fighting over who has claim over this bride, the young woman dies of shame. There's some question as to whether it's a literal death, though (ancient mythologies weren't expertly edited, it seems). Finnabair reappears in the last paragraph of the epic and marries the warrior Cúchulainn.

Whether they enjoyed a relationship with their daughter or not, which seems unlikely as Finnabair is married to their sworn enemy, Medb and Ailill live in a state of passionate conflict that was peaceful enough... Until Ailill kills his wife's lover, Fergus, and then Medb contracts with another hero to murder her equally unfaithful husband. Legend has it that Medb met her end while taking a bath in a lovely outdoor pool. She was slain by her own nephew (allegedly the queen had killed her own sister) with a "brain ball" to the head.

The Pricey Contradictions of the Crown

Oh, Medb, was it worth it? Were you just terrifically misunderstood? Was there more to this war than some pillow talk about livestock that got blown all out of proportion? Was the death toll just the Dark Ages' equivalent of fake news? Can we adore you for your brashness and your passion and ignore the body count? Can we look past your faults and love you for the mere fact that you existed and that your story made it across the barren stretches of time when women were written out of nearly every history inscribed on vellum, scroll, and printed page?

Irish language poet Nuala Ní Dhomhnaill thought it was all worth it. In her poem that starts this chapter, she placed the worth of Medb's dignity above all the bulls and the bullshit and let the Queen of Connacht be our feminist icon. Together, Nuala and Medb lead us modern-day poetry readers—and wannabe Amazons—across the land, that land that is meant to be as sacred as a goddess's body, as a woman's body.

Maybe it's because she only writes in Irish, or maybe it's the way the fairy magic glints in her eyes, but to me, Nuala herself has always been more of an otherworldly goddess than a queen. An approachable, otherworldly goddess whom I once accosted at 5AM in the Dublin Airport, to be specific. There she was, also waiting to catch that early morning flight to Boston, her eyes full of more squint than glint in the fluorescent lights of the terminal. I called out her name as I frantically unzipped my luggage. Somewhere near the bottom of my bag was her latest edition of poetry and, of course, I needed her to sign it for me. Perhaps she's just famous enough and her fans are just crazy enough that this thing happens from time to time. In all honesty, I hope she vaguely remembers that American redhead with the passion for poetry when she queues up for the departure gate, even after all these years.

I know that I need to remember Nuala. I need to remember how she doesn't just defend Medb but actually lets the fiery queen speak through her. And, my goddess, does she have good reasons. In other parts of the poem, she curses the "twenty-pint heroes" who slobber and grab as if a woman's body is theirs to dominate. Medb was willing to wage war on the field to defend her Sovereignty. Nuala, who transformed the old boys' club of Irish poetry, is willing to wage war on the page to defend an ancient queen, and also to speak for every woman who has had enough of the machismo and the casual abuse. Nuala and Medb awaken me to something I don't want to admit: I'm so much more likely to be the princess who wants to appease and smile politely and make peace at my own expense. They remind me it's my right, my privilege, and my obligation to speak up for myself, to fight for myself, and to take up the crown.

Oh, how terrible the queen can be. Oh, how glorious, necessary, and complicated. When it all comes down to it, the queen's contradictions are just a reflection of our terribly perplexing world. She is only as fierce and brutal as the situation unfolding around her requires her to be. When I am afraid of the queen and her raised voice and her raised sword, it's just a sign that I am afraid of the cruelty of our culture and the unpredictability of our natural world. It's also a sign that I am afraid of the power within me.

Part of my own conflict with the queen comes from the misogynist within. (Yes, of course even the feminists have internalized misogyny when raised in the patriarchal smog.) When we tell the story of Medb and ask her to illuminate our queen archetype, we're stepping up to tell a difficult story. Maybe you see a bold, sex-positive icon who can beat the lads at their own game. You might be too distracted by the greed, materialism, and narcissistic bloodshed to love the iconoclastic heroine. But then, we live in a time that embraces both versions of the narrative. We live in a "be a nice girl, but also dress the right kind of sexy, and tune into *Game of Thrones*" culture that preaches compliance, creativity, and consumerism, and celebrates really big explosions all at the same time. Larger-than-life narratives seem to be designed to inspire us to action, but they tend to numb us into becoming spectators who live tweet the actors' every move. And, of course gendered double standards abound. When male characters perpetuate violence they look like heroes, but when women act similarly they look like madwomen or cartoons. Though we live in an era teeming with more dragon queens and female superheroes than ever before, we have not yet elected a woman president in the United States. The powerful woman is still too threatening and too strange. She's too much and not enough woman all at the same time. Medb is all of these. And the queen within you probably is, too.

We could linger in the pop culture arcade for eternity as we try to sort through all these contradictory narratives, choices, and role models but here's the long and the short of it: We need aspects of the queen to help us get things done in the world, be it making money, making a meal, or making babies. Depending on the moment in history, we need women to make war and peace, too. There's a lot that each of us needs to do to decode the queen energy in our lives, and there are a lot of different ways her powers can manifest, but there's one thing that is universal: The queen gets it done. If she doesn't get it done, she's not the queen.

The Cool, Confident Queen and Her Cold, Calculating Shadow

At long last, I feel like I am figuring out how to hold the queen—lightly, but with a level of passionate intensity and cool, confident mastery (at least some of the time).

When I am at my best, I can avail myself of her gifts—creation, birth, manifestation, leadership, commitment, responsibility, structure, righteous rage, passionate change, protection, nurturing, stability, balance. I can mother children, make sure everyone eats a green vegetable, and make sure that more money comes in than goes out each month. I can stand up against bullies, be they overbearing soccer coaches, unreasonable clients, or the politician motivated only by corporate lobbyists.

Though Medb's story is one of sex and violence, the typical superpowers of the modern queen look a lot like "adulting." Formal contracts, dealing with authority figures, and nearly all activities related to housekeeping are part of the queen's domain. Such things make my skin crawl, and yet, spreadsheets, reading the fine print, dealing with bankers, cops, and doctors, and vacuuming are inherent parts of modern life. The queen knows how to deal with all of it—and can even thrive in the process. And when she really just doesn't have the requisite time, attention, and elbow grease to keep up with scrubbing the tub or do the admin tasks, she makes a bit more money so she can pay someone a fair wage to do the task.

When I can stand assuredly in my queen energy, I am able to figure out which rules I need to follow, what red tape is just waiting to be sliced up with a machete (or some safety scissors from the kids' art cabinet), and what rules are just waiting to be reformed and rewritten. She is my inner executive, and she always makes the life insurance payments on time. The queen knows that conscious entrepreneurship, ethical politics, enlightened medicine, and compassionate education are possible, and she's ready to raise the right kind of ruckus to make them all a reality.

But then, there is the aspect of the queen that isn't all that interested in reform. This is the version of the queen who likes power for the sake of power, whether she earns it through her own hard work and initiative, or whether she came by her position by luck of birth and marriage. The shadowy side of the queen is on display in every woman who hasn't just been subtly infected with misogyny but who has been subsumed by it and becomes a handmaid of the patriarchy. Becoming one with the dark elements that fathered her (though her actual dad may have been a peach), she will side with the oppressors, voting against her own right to choose, to get healthcare, to be paid a fair wage. If this sounds a bit like the rhetoric you hear from the progressives who talk freely about the white women who voted to put a racist sexual predator in the Oval Office, it's meant to. The queen can be a fantastically powerful force for good, whose positive leadership can elevate a small family, a growing company, or an entire nation. The queen can also win her place through her blindness, her complicity, and her naked willingness to conspire against the Sovereignty of others—especially when she has the good old boy network on her side.

The shadowy side of the queen flashes across my life, especially if I am feeling threatened, insecure, or inferior for some reason. I may not be promising my daughters to random kings in hopes of winning my feckless war like Medb, but I can be all sorts of entangled with her unhealthy patterns: controlling, self-sacrificing, scarcity-driven, power-hungry, defensive, judgmental, self-absorbed, and manipulative. There is a part of me that wants so much to be in charge, who is desperate to be in control of everything that surrounds me. There is a part of me that feels she's achieved enough, endured enough, and waited long enough to deserve it. But the wise part of me knows that's the talk of a fraud. It's also the talk of the privileged. To be a white, middle-class, highly educated, able-bodied, cis-gendered female is to be totally aware of the abundance and possibility available, and yet feel a degree of powerlessness at the same time. It feels ridiculous, impossible, and valid all at once. When you're raised a white girl and emerge into white womanhood, you have permission to be queen of so much, but the patriarchal systems still rig the game so you spend vast amounts of time feeling small. The limitations placed upon women by the white supremacist patriarchy are real. Rather than allowing that to paralyze you, remember that you're crowning the queen within so you have the stamina and guts to change the system.

The Sovereignty Knot's queen is different from the kind of queen that's celebrated in much of our modern culture. Chances are, the queen you've been taught to admire and emulate is part of a system that is inherently hierarchical and repressive. We all learned "the system" in our own way, whether from parents, teachers, or the media. You probably weren't schooled in the ways of the white supremacist patriarchy in an overt way. Instead, it was all part of "the way things were." Maybe you were raised inside the bubble of privilege like I was, or maybe you watched from the outside, never part of it, but always hyper-aware of it. With Sovereignty comes an awareness that you have a choice. You can choose to work within the established power structures that put white men at the top and only promote people of other races, genders, and sexualities who are willing to play by their rules. Or, you can choose to forge a new path and work to transform the inequality as you encounter it.

When you're born white, straight, and healthy in America, you generally have the illusion of another choice. You can choose not to see racism and all the other injustices visited on people who don't fit the majority's mold. When you decide to invest in the kind of Sovereignty I'm talking about, you realize you don't want to unsee the reality of the world, even if the accident of your birth makes that possible. You don't want to rule over the world as it is: You want to help create the world as it could be.

We're not trying to make the crown into another status symbol. Rather, we see the crown as a Sovereign symbol that reminds you of the power you've always possessed. You become a leader who is so comfortable with your power that you gracefully pass the crown to the next person who needs to awaken to their Sovereignty, and then you realize you never gave up a thing.

Meet Your Queen

To be the queen is to balance the way you care for yourself and the way you care for the world.

The queen of the Sovereignty Knot is inspired by a desire to serve people and the planet, not just by personal profit. Whether you're in a traditional caregiver role as a parent, a teacher, or a child of an elderly parent, or you're called to help others in a different way, the queen within you is motivated by a need to shepherd, steward, and foster. The queen knows how to deal with money managers and power brokers, and she can manage her own money and broker her own power. Though you might freeze up the moment you open your bank statement, the queen within you is ready to learn. The queen is the one who helps ensure you're in a relationship with a partner who is your equal, with a person who can respond to your needs. She's the one who helps you satisfy your own needs whether you're in partnership or on your own. For all the ways the queen archetype has been twisted in our culture, she is part of this mighty trinity because we need her pragmatic abilities, her nurturing grace, and her desire to offer everyone a sense of safety and prosperity.

At her best, she takes us through and beyond all the toxic masculinity and whitewashing of society and balances gratitude for all that is with the soul-deep desire to change the world. So how do we do all this? How do we balance the tremendous variety of practical magic and inspirational leadership that we require from the queen? How do we help her uncover her own blind spots so she isn't repeating the mistakes of the patriarchy and calling it feminist empowerment merely because she's a woman?

Just as the princess asked us to tune into the spirits of forgiveness and celebration so we could fully embrace her power, the queen asks us to explore two new energies with a couple of writing prompts that invite us to tune into gratitude and desire. When fully expressed and in relationship with the princess and the wise woman within, the queen is the ultimate mistress of balance. If anyone can handle polar opposites—like being a passionate changemaker and the nurturing mother while trying to navigate a world that has been rigged in favor of maintaining the status quo—it's her.

The Queen Considers Gratitude

You've made gratitude lists before. Maybe you're like me and you've made them in your head because you were too busy putting more creative, more urgent ideas on paper. This time, however, you're asked to consider gratitude with the energy of the queen.

You know that you are in the Sovereignty Knot of relationship with all these aspects of yourself. You know that you are bound in knots of relationship with countless people on the emotional, professional, and communal level. You know that you are intimately tied to all the systems in our environment, from breathable air to potable water to the solid earth beneath your feet. Knowing you are part of such a vast web, what are you truly grateful for?

Writing Prompt: Gratitude

It's time to actually sit down and put your gratitude list on paper. Please don't skip out on this because it feels too basic. The queen gets things done. If she doesn't get things done, she's not the queen. And you, my friend, are here to be *queen*.

Make one great big master list. Allow yourself to marinate in the magic of gratefulness and consider making this a weekly or even daily practice.

And then take this one step further. When you have made the list of the *what*, also lean into the *why* of everything you are grateful for. When you give yourself the time and space to understand why you feel the way you do, you give yourself permission to fully inhabit your own life. The queen is an outward-facing archetype, but her power is rooted in a deep understanding of her own inner world.

The Queen Considers Desire

The other half of the queen's equation is desire. It's a more complicated concept than it might seem at first glance. It's a simple question to form—"What do you want?"—but as Ragnell, Arthur, and Gawain showed us, it can take a great deal of time and discernment to find the real answer. And even once you have an answer like "Sovereignty," the quest has only just begun. Sovereignty looks different for all of us, after all.

I would never expect to offer up a writing prompt with the phrase, "write into what you truly desire," and think a writer would come up with the answers immediately. Desire is a longer, slipperier story than gratitude. It calls into account every fiber of who you are. The search for your truest desires requires that you interrogate all those "false desires" that have been layered on you based on others' expectations and social conditioning.

It took more than a decade of married life for me to realize that my romantic relationship with my husband wasn't the most important thing in my life. It wasn't possible to put our love affair front and center forever, but it also wasn't even something that I *wanted*. When I realized I'd unconsciously pegged my happiness on the satisfaction of an outdated desire, I needed to mourn for a little while. Then I could let that go and I could *breathe*. I was free to devote myself to uncovering my desires in that moment of life, and I could get to the work of satisfying them.

Writing Prompt: Desire

Sit down with the intention to get to the heart of your desires. You might find yourself writing about love, power, or freedom. You might end up writing about sex, money, or politics. It's all allowed as long as it's true for you. You might write about living by the ocean, quitting your job, or being closer to your grandchildren.

As Natalie Goldberg, the founding mother of writing practice says, "Go for the jugular."[11] Write from the place that exists beneath the veneer of appearances, the source of your late-night truths and your most primal longing.

Write for at least twenty minutes without stopping. At the end of your writing session, ask yourself if your true desires appear on the page. It may take several sessions to pull back the layers of the onion to get to what you really want and now what you think you *should* want.

---

11 Natalie Goldberg, *Writing Down the Bones* (Boston: Shambhala, 1986), 8.

The Territory of the Queen: The Castle

When I thought of the territory of the queen, I knew it had to be a castle. But which one? I'd seen plenty back when I was a student conquering Europe with a backpack and a *Let's Go* guidebook, but they were just someone else's ruins. For me, the cliffs and the cave are very specific and feel intimate and knowable, even if they're remote places I'll only visit a handful of times. The castle refused to take shape, even in my imagination. That's when I realized I was leaning into memory and fantasy when all I had to do was look around the room.

The castle of the queen is the real world you've created around you in this moment. It's the tiny apartment, the raised ranch full of Fisher Price toys, the beach house you've worked so hard to buy. This is the place where the action of daily life happens, with all of its mundane tasks and all of its dedicated love. In the best scenario, when you walk into your castle you can feel both safe and free. Even if your home has been taken over by a family's growing mountain of stuff, you want to be able to say "bless this mess" with a smile on your face rather than endlessly cursing the chaos. If you feel less powerful and less happy the moment you walk through the door it's important to remember that, as the queen, you have the power to transform your living situation.

Once upon a time, a castle was forever. It took lifetimes to build, so you weren't going to up and move because you wanted to be part of the new up-and-coming neighborhood. This modern ability to pick up and start fresh is revolutionary. We have a chance to become Sovereign in new territory, establishing a new relationship with a new stretch of land. The essence of the queen is to bloom where she is planted, to become fully at home upon the patch of the planet she walks each day—not as the ruler, but as the keeper, the observer, and the caretaker. The queen's power to occupy and heal a space is as vast as her potential territory. She can use this power to design a gorgeous, elegant living space or to build a nest where her children and their friends can feel welcome. It can be a place to read books long into the night, spend long mornings making love, or to share long, lavish meals. Her castle can be her own refuge from the work she does to make the wider world a better place.

Writing Prompt: The Castle and Your Map of Sovereignty

Again, pull out your own Sovereignty Map. The cliffs and the cave have their place in life, but the castle is the place where you can rest and come back to yourself. Whether you're a homebody or a woman who loves to wander, consider whether it feels right to place your castle at the center fo the map.

Describe this castle, lingering on the atmosphere of the space and how being there makes you feel. Is the castle on your Sovereignty Map a reflection of your reality or a "someday" dream? There is no wrong answer here, but that answer does reveal a great deal.

If, as you write, you find that your current home really does feel like a suitable castle for a Sovereign being like you, notice that and celebrate that. How can you deepen your relationship with the land upon which you live? How can you further open your home to welcome others so it becomes a space for connection?

If you realize that your living situation isn't fit for a queen—or, more specifically, for a woman on a Sovereignty quest—then it's time to write into what needs to change. Consider whether the next step in your Sovereignty journey includes moving, redecorating, or asking someone to leave and find their own place. Ultimately, you want your castle to be a place where you can feel both safe and free.

As you look at your map, also think about landmarks that are important to your queen. Is there a field where she did battle? Is there a gathering place where she organized a committee of like minds? The queen's power may be focused at home, but she also does tremendous work in the wider world.

CHAPTER 8

Negotiating Sovereignty and Motherhood

I've never forgotten to pick up the girls from school, but I almost forgot to write this chapter. In the initial conception of this book, "Sovereignty and motherhood" was always on the list. But then, during a year of drafting and rearranging, all sorts of other topics proved more essential and intriguing than this mommying thing. Without thinking, I relegated the work that consumed my thirties to some sort of extracurricular activity that deserved merely a passing mention in chapters that delved into the "real" stuff that influences women's power, potential, and self-worth. This is the power of the patriarchy, my sisters. This distorted,

159 &

dangerous worldview causes the people who birth and care for children to minimize their labor and their love until it becomes little more than a footnote in the hustle for something more... real. Why do we lose track of our lived reality? Because we've been taught that "real" means quantifiable, front-page worthy, and directly related to the increase of the GDP.

In truth, motherhood is at the core of my Sovereignty story, but I had to dig through a hundred thousand words of other people's expectations to tell you that I was forged by this ordinary phenomenon of parenting. Because someone started calling me "Mom," my illusions dissolved and my endurance was revealed. My cauldron of patience and strength has proved deeper than I thought possible because every sleepless night gave way to a morning when I had to suck it up and be nice. Fortunately, the catastrophes that unfolded when that strength ran dry have been more revelatory than terrible. Fortunately, patience seems to be a renewable resource even though I often don't understand where it keeps coming from. Fortunately, there was always a beacon of Sovereignty on a distant horizon that reminded me not to lose myself in all smiling and surviving.

There's been no choice but to grow and evolve in the face of my children's natural and perpetual demands. These girls have relied on my resilience and my power, and I've had no choice but to find new supplies of my own Sovereign strength. I've known this at some visceral, mama lioness level from the very start, but all that conditioning and distraction got in the way of claiming all the wonder, drama, and trauma of being Mother. The relentless pursuit of "more" made me blind to how "just" being a mom had made me into one hell of a phenomenal woman.

And yet, what if I hadn't had kids? What if I'd had the freedom to meet people, make art, and make choices like someone without the blessed burden of dependents? Wouldn't I have found another path to Sovereignty? Of course. Sovereignty was always my destination, just as it is for every woman who values her own self-worth over the weight of oppression, distraction, and destruction. So, if I didn't spend so much time responding to the "Mo-om, I'm done!" that got hollered from the bathroom every time a small child pooped, what other forms of creative innovation would have emerged? Would I still be dragging myself to a day job, spending weekends on the couch with a stack of books, underlining like my life depended on it and hoping someday I would have the courage to write my own? Or would I have published my own stack of books by now? I have no idea. That's not the story I am living or telling, and since I've never regretted the decision to become a mother for any longer than an exhausted afternoon at a time, I'm not interested in the question for my own sake. And yet, there are millions of women in the world who will never have children, either because they can't or don't wish to. Certainly Sovereignty doesn't rely on birthing babies or raising kids. There are as many paths to Sovereignty as there are creatures who've decided to take on the challenge, after all.

So, motherhood isn't an essential ingredient in the Sovereignty brew, and women with children can definitely find their own paths to Sovereignty in the midst of the mommying. One question remains: Do women with children become Sovereign *because of* or *in spite of* motherhood?

For modern mothers, the ambivalence is real. And it is spectacular. Are they making us into superwomen or are they growing bundles of kryptonite, here to drain us of our power with everything from sweet baby sighs to teenage rebellions? Spend three seconds on any modern American mother's social media feed to see the memes roll by. *Oh, you fantastic, amazing children, we adore you. Oh, you burdensome brood, we've been vanquished by you. We would die for you, but we just can't get up off the couch to cook one more goddamn pot of mac 'n cheese for you.* There are women in opposing camps, to be sure, but the reality is in the messy slide across the spectrum between soul-deep attachment and soul-shredding claustrophobia.

Our proud and weary devotion is well celebrated, and it even predates the internet. George Bernard Shaw once said, "Being a mother means that your heart is no longer yours; it wanders wherever your children do." Forgive me for not chasing down the context for that line. I saw it on Facebook. It doesn't actually matter what an Irish playwright thought of motherhood one hundred years ago or whether the character who said it was being canonized or pitied for her sacrifice. What matters is that this sentiment still resonates. We live in a society where it's a badge of honor to ship your heart off on the kindergarten bus or to the freshman dorm and still manage to stay alive. Funny how raising a kid makes it necessary to give up a vital organ. This sacrificial arrangement seems rather strange and cruel, but we seem to keep replicating it and the species continues to survive. But what does this do to the individual women who are caught up in such expectations?

Sovereignty, my sister-mothers: We're starving for it. We're afraid of it. We aren't sure if we lost it or if we had it at all. No matter how long we've been playing the game, it's still unclear exactly how we're supposed to be Sovereign and be somebody's mom at the same time. It's also unclear whether we should take parenting advice from long-dead Irishmen. Collectively, we still aren't sure if it's possible to be a good enough mother if we maintain something as selfish and necessary as our own freedom, strength, emotional equanimity, and personal space.

These women who want it all and then forget to want anything at all in the midst of the service and the exhaustion and the love… you are my people. We are overwhelmed, overcommitted maternal forces of nature caught between a radiant passion for our offspring and the madness that emerges in the face of the endless demands for everything from hugs to lunch money to their old room back after graduation. For us, Sovereignty depends on connecting with that essential, enduring self that comes before and after any identity acquired through the relationship with someone else.

To this point, I've spent well over 3,500 days in the presence of my progeny. Caring for them has swallowed the vast majority of my waking hours. Countless hours of sleep have been stolen by nightmares, wet beds, and desperate mouths searching out one breast and then another until dawn. This has been my reality, all diaper bags and crayon art and multiplication tables, but I tried to leave it out of the story of my life. In the midst of it all, I would hide in my office to type one more paragraph and skimp on rest to revise one more page. I would push past mental and emotional exhaustion to show up on social media to say something inspirational or witty or to merely prove I was present in the world. Every minute of my writing time has been stolen from kids—either because I've denied them a measure of my care and attention when I chose to write or because I decided to spend time on my own words rather than on the business I've built to support my family. For all mothers of young children, creative acts are seditious acts against the regime of motherhood. Even if you have a sleeping infant or a remarkably well-behaved preschooler who is happy to draw while you write, the magic of making something can only happen when the planets and the naptime align. If you are someone with access to childcare, either because your mom lives down the street or you've got the resources to pay someone "just" so you can be creative, it still takes deliberation and energy to arrange it. After all that begging, borrowing, and stealing to get some time and space to yourself, what's more real—the relentless responsibilities of caregiving or the rare and delicious escape into a forbidden creative world?

This isn't meant to be a martyr's song of resentment. My love is vaster than my ambivalence, and it has been from the moment I sat at a cafe squinting over my 2009 datebook to calculate just how late my period was. From that moment onward, my biological need to create another human life wildly outstripped my artistic desire to write something. But now that I am in the phase of tending children rather than making them from scratch, my attention has expanded and shifted to include creative as well as procreative acts. The act of pushing children into the world— both times wedged into the tiny alcove in our bathroom, my husband straddling the toilet tank to hold me under the arms while our midwife knelt at my feet to catch the baby—that was an act of fierce, wild Sovereignty. Ten years ago, it seemed a bit radical to eschew the safety of a typical maternity ward for the wonderful, unsterile field that is our own home. Home birth has become so completely normal to me at this point, I realize I'm not sure if the culture has shifted toward accepting midwifery and natural childbirth or if it's just me that has changed. I have so completely lived and embodied that decision to give birth at home on my own terms that I barely remember to mention it in my Sovereignty story.

Pause here. This is something we need to remark upon and realize: When we live our story so fully, when we drop the doubt and the endless inner chatter and exchange it for a quiet form of Sovereign power, we may actually *stop* seeing the significance of our own choices and victories. The true Sovereign carries her power effortlessly and generously shares it with others in service to the greater good, but she must always remember the distinct, glorious nature of that power. If you don't remember and honor your power, no one else will either.

Motherhood has become the lens through which I see the world, and so I stopped noticing it the way you stop noticing the glasses balanced on your nose. If that is what Shaw was trying to say with that wandering heart comment, I suppose I must agree with him. Being Mom is so very integral to my identity that I usually cannot see it as the magical force that it is. Even my own body seems more separate from me than my role as mother to my two girls. I nearly forgot to include motherhood in the Sovereignty Knot because my children are wound so completely into my heart, my consciousness, and my routine. But even if my days revolve around my kids, and nearly every choice I make needs to take them into account, this quest for Sovereignty demands that I remember that my power derives from motherhood. And, at the same time, the Sovereign in me knows that my children are *not* my life force.

I love you, girls, but Mama's got a big old beating heart of her own. And I've got to honor mine so that I can teach you to honor yours.

You Can Carry More Than One Heart In Your Body, But Only One Is Yours

There's that Mary Oliver poem, "Wild Geese," in which she says, "You only have to let the soft animal of your body love what it loves." It was only when I held my daughters in my arms for the first time that I finally understood that. And it would rearrange everything for a good long time.

Since day one, these kids were destined to come before my creative and professional advancement. It didn't have to be this way—other mothers are built differently and everyone still manages to grow up safe, happy, and whole. This just seems to be the way I'm wired. When I was pregnant with our older daughter and my husband and I were visiting daycares, I chose to hear the voice in me that screamed, "No. Just no. H-E-double-L no will my baby get lined up in one of those little seats and learn how to take a bottle from a stranger." Though I could have labeled that quaking in my belly as a cute baby kick or a trick of the digestion, I left each facility feeling shaken to my core. I tend to be allergic to written agreements, especially when it comes to something as organic as responding to the needs of an infant. Sending my two-month-old to a place with regulations and release forms seemed impossible.

My entire reaction to motherhood shocked me, frankly. Though I was better at professing it than living it to the letter, my feminism has always relied on a woman's right to work and her right to autonomy. Suddenly, whether it was related to childcare, co-sleeping, or baby-wearing, I was making choice after choice that would keep me as close as possible to my child. There was barely any room for daylight between us at all once I quit my job.

Motherhood would demand I become fiercely practical in a host of new ways, and so my queen had plenty to do after she stopped trying to manage her part of the college library. At the same time, motherhood was my first opportunity to operate by pure instinct—damn the schedules, the contracts, and the dictates of the how-to manuals. As a mom, I would write the rules and break them, following the wildness of the princess and the sagacity of the wise woman as much as I engaged with the stable, nurturing energy of the queen. None of it seemed like a real choice at the time. One foot just followed the other. One need was satisfied and the next appeared.

Even as my need to be seen as "more than just mom" emerged, it was quickly submerged by love, duty, and the all-encompassing adventure of motherhood. And yet, my Sovereign self endured. If anything, she was growing under the surface to become a dozen times more formidable. To make that happen, my definition of Sovereignty had to change. Perhaps you'd say it had to mature. Rather than being about independence, being the best, or being the supreme ruler of the station wagon or even my daily routine, Sovereignty in motherhood is about consciously integrating all parts of yourself. As I was invited—and forced—to stand in my own peaceful, passionate power, I was embodying my Sovereignty more fully than I ever had before.

Though the queen is most likely to be occupied with the work of caregiving, it wouldn't be fair to stick "mothering" in her category and allow the princess and the wise woman to exist unencumbered on either side of the child-rearing years. Remember, the power of these archetypes exists in their ability to loop across the lifetime and we're being called to think and live beyond that old construction of maid-mother-crone. The queen's ability to mother is only as effective as the support she gains from the other elements of our Sovereignty trinity. All too many of us rely on the queen within to be in charge of "all the things," and we end up drinking huge cups of bitterness—and red wine—to deal with the loneliness and the exhaustion.

My queen may rule over birth and creation and she might be able to pack a school lunch before she even has caffeine, but I need the princess to save me from mom jeans. I also need the princess to remind me that it's okay to let my children listen to Katy Perry's "Roar" a hundred times on repeat because these are the first crucial ingredients of girl power. The princess bids me to hold my tongue even when my fifth grader is oblivious to time, my repeated requests, or oncoming traffic because she has her nose in a book. The princess holds up the mirror and lets me see myself in these girls. And it's her energy I use to forgive both my daughters and myself for being absentminded and self-absorbed in the face of deadlines and real-world concerns.

And the wise woman is there to be the omniscient, though invisible, grandmother who sees and soothes the friction that inevitably rises between daughters and their mother, between the princess and the queen within all women. The wise woman understands everyone's language because she's used all these words before. She holds the insults and overly expressive sighs and works her magic to diffuse their impact. Maybe she's the one who gets everyone to call a truce while baking muffins together. Maybe she gets everyone to stop bickering amongst themselves long enough to make signs for the next climate action event the family will attend together. It's the wise woman who holds the spirit of reverence so that everyone can stop arguing and take in the wonder of a dragonfly, the antics of the family cats, or the scope of real suffering in the world. The wise woman is beyond the struggle for individuation that rages within the princess. She is not obsessed with her to-do list the way the queen is. The wise woman simply holds the space for everyone to settle into who they really are so the group can create a new way of being.

When, in the presence of the children we're put here to raise, we can call on all these elements within us, something magical happens: Sovereignty happens, if we let it. It's as ironic and impossible sounding as it is true. There are so many ways to awaken to Sovereignty. For me, right now, it's this mind-body-soul endeavor that is motherhood, with all its distractions, exhaustion, indignities, and limitless love. Motherhood has been the laboratory in which I've developed the alchemical skills of turning doubt into getting it done and "maybe someday" into "yes, it's time." It's where I have learned to trust myself and trust that I could shape some small part of the world as I crafted a culture of love and acceptance inside my small family.

What if, instead of seeing the endless drudgery of motherhood with its piles of laundry and sibling squabbles, we understood that doing the work to raise a kid is also an opportunity to raise up yourself? When you're "just mom," it's too easy to start believing that your singular flower has had its day, been composted, and turned into the soil that is merely meant to anchor the next season's blooms. What if you *knew* you were more than the cook, chauffeur, and playdate planner? What if you were consciously living into another chapter of your Sovereignty story, especially during this longest shortest time of parenting young humans?

We Become Sovereign by Conveying Sovereignty

Think back to the Sovereignty Goddess in the cave, who constantly passed on her power and so became stronger in the process. As we initiate another human into this life, so, too, are we initiated into our own becoming. When I began to see motherhood as an initiation rather than an inevitable rite of passage or a long study in sleep deprivation, I was able to convey that power to my kids with minimal resentment or fear that giving to them would automatically deplete me.

Day to day, this endeavor is more like an excruciating endurance contest than a pleasant field trip to some mystical crystal cave. Writing this book, building a business, and fitting in some yoga and some cardio has had to happen in, around, and beyond the company of my children. So many days, I have sat down at the desk cranky and bleary-eyed because a snuggle-seeking preschooler stole my sleep yet again. I have had to find the words through the haze of frustration and the creativity at the bottom of yet another pot of strong black coffee. Whether it's because Mama is writing a book or because Mama is simply trying to maintain a sense of self on the other side of bringing up baby, Sovereignty is a constant negotiation. But it's not an impossible one.

When I can lift myself out of the story of what's impossible because I'm trapped in the frumpy grind that is getting children out of the house each day, I can look back on a decade of staggering growth that happened not in spite of, and maybe not fully because of, but certainly right alongside the development of two creatures who are already drawing portraits of their own Sovereignty archetypes (though to the untrained eye they look like simple drawings of fairies, witches, and women in ball gowns).

For practicality's sake (because there's no such thing as Sovereignty theory when it comes to motherhood, only Sovereignty praxis), let's close this chapter with a hike my five-year-old and I took on a recent summer Saturday. This was a sweet, necessary morning following an endless week pockmarked by 3AM visits from this very same thirsty, lonesome, monster-fearing child. While most of our walk was devoted to seeking gnome holes and dodging spiderwebs and carefully exploring an old creepy cabin we found far out in the woods, I switched the conversation to more serious, real-world topics as the trail looped back to the car. I mentioned the particularly draining session of bedtime pyrotechnics we'd all suffered through the night before. I'd lain with her in the dark, waiting for sleep for what felt like an eternity to me and "not enough snuggles!" to her. Eventually I did leave her bed, my own useful energy waning and the weight of all I still had to accomplish that evening heavy on my mind. She had cried herself into a sweaty sleep long after I said goodnight to her.

"Mairead, my love, we need to talk about bedtime tonight." She wouldn't exactly acknowledge me, but she seemed to be listening. "Being your mama is one of the most important jobs I could do." (Yes, I was very conscious that I did not say *the* most important job because I refuse to distill my life down to one single calling.) "But I think you understand that Mama has other jobs too, right?

You know I have my book to write and my clients to help, right? You know that Mama also needs exercise and meditation and her own sleep too, right?"

She didn't answer, but I knew I was saying this as much for myself as I was for her. "I love you with my whole entire heart," I continued, "And I will promise to give you all my love before you go to bed and when you wake up in the morning. And I need you to promise that you will hold that love in your heart, even when I have to leave the room to do my other work, okay?"

Did it make a difference? She did sleep easily, at least for the next few nights. And I had some sort of new working vocabulary— that was even kid friendly!—that described my quest to be princess, queen, and wise woman all in one day. It's my job to maintain a conscious relationship with all that I have to hold, all that I have to do, all that supports my spirit. It's not about choosing between motherhood, work, romance, or even self-care. It's about realizing that as important as they all are, none are more essential than my Sovereignty.

Writing Prompt: Your Mothering Story

Whether you have birthed and/or raised children or not, you have a mothering story. Because mothering is so closely aligned with a woman's experience, both having and not having children are key parts of your Sovereignty story.

Who have you mothered? What was that experience for you and what do you imagine it was like for them? Can you imagine Sovereignty and motherhood existing side by side and even becoming allies?

You might already know that you would be able to fill a book with your mothering experiences. Or, you might be like me, and, for one reason or another, you may have pushed the mommy stuff off to one side and are just diving into the details of your mother story for the first time. Give this story the space it requires and remember what you've already learned about forgiveness, celebration, gratitude, and desire as you tell your story of motherhood.

CHAPTER 9

A Crow, a Church, and the Story
of Little Soul

The trinity formed by the tall pillar candle, the arched window with its bold and perfect panes, and the golden cross with its sunburst center had a nice symmetry to it. It offered a place for my eyes to rest when I was weary of staring at Christ on the cross, the symbol of divine suffering that loomed over it all. It was easier to sit through Mass with some attitude of prayerfulness when I looked at these steady objects and not the awkward preteen altar girls who would never get promoted beyond choir director in a place like this.

And then I looked beyond my well-honed feminist criticism of the Catholic Church and tried to stop interrogating the faith that had been at the center of my family's life for generations. Through a distant window, I could see a single crow perched on a naked winter tree. She threw herself into a silent scream, her body rocking with a call that echoed deep inside my own chest. It had been more than twenty years since I had left walled-in religious spaces like these and joined the birds, calling up to Father God in the limitless sky and whispering to the Mother Goddess in the enduring earth. Yet here I was during a Sunday Mass in a prosperous enclave of semi-rural New Jersey. My daughters sat between my ninety-six-year-old grandfather and me. I did the bare minimum to get non-indoctrinated kids to sit quietly and quit playing with the kneeler and the missals. Most of my attention was directed at a sensation between my breasts that was somewhere between the buzz of spiritual energy and a gathering storm of fear. Considering the circumstances, you might have blamed this strange feeling on lingering traces of Catholic guilt.

Prayer and meditation are part of my daily life. I have spent more than a decade studying energy healing and spiritual practice at a place called the Sacred Center Mystery School, where "you can't make this stuff up" expansions in consciousness happen all the time. It was just strange that something similar was happening in a church. I'd spent years telling anyone who seemed to care about why I abandoned my childhood religion that I never found it possible to reach the divine inside a building with a bunch of people mumbling in unison.

My departure from the family religion was a good-natured, noisy one fueled by my emerging feminist consciousness. It wasn't just the patriarchal oppression—though that was a huge factor, of course. I also resented being nudged along a spiritual path that felt completely devoid of magic. This is rather amusing, considering it was the Catholic Church I wanted to leave. They have weeping statues, exorcisms, and bodies that don't decay, for crying out loud! This was an organization that actively advocated for miracles of all kinds, be it a spontaneous healing or the occasional levitating saint. That wasn't my experience growing up in the CCD classes of the eighties though. At the Confraternity of Christian Doctrine (after spending more than ten years attending it, I had no idea what "CCD" meant until I Googled it a minute ago), they foisted banal pictures of a pasty-faced Jesus upon us and constantly urged us to "spread the good news" (whatever that was). It felt like some sort of vague invitation to be a nice person who reminded their parents to take them to Mass. Sex and the body were forbidden, too, of course, but that was all left unspoken. Our particular generation was born of hippies who washed up on the shores of Cape Cod to avoid the rat race. This Catholicism was riddled with contradiction and was generally of the "show up, stay quiet, and vote Democrat" kind. The Kennedys attended our church, after all.

That kind of moral hypocrisy was fine with me because I never really expected the Church to teach me right and wrong. I was more troubled that none of their obligatory prayers and proscribed holy days got me any closer to the divine. As my mom put it, "You kids were practically raised Protestant." If you knew my mother, this random statement, which could be interpreted as obtuse or even offensive, made perfect sense and wasn't meant to be a slight on any Episcopalians or Lutherans I might meet on the school bus. She knew what I craved, and it was something like the mysticism and sacred mystery she got in her fifties and sixties parochial schools. My mother also got the everyday cruelty of the nuns and heaping helpings of self-loathing, too, of course, so it's clear that I ultimately got the better deal. All I needed to do was give myself permission to go outside and put my feet in the dirt and look inside to the galaxy of divinity within to find a hundred lifetimes' worth of mystical truth.

If my family was aggrieved by my decision to leave Catholicism behind, they've largely kept it to themselves. Every now and again, someone will get wistful about the next generation's membership in the Church, but their vaguely expressed disappointment is nothing compared to the psychological warfare waged on my mom by the sisters from the convent. And it was nothing compared to the flurry of condemnation I was about to conjure inside my head.

An Outdated Inheritance of Shame

As I have carved out my own spiritual path, Mass is now a rare familial duty that must be endured from time to time. On this particular February morning, however, I seemed to be having an actual religious experience in a place that a whole lot of people considered "the house of the Lord." After so many years of fighting them, I just wasn't used to fitting in so well with the crowd. It was making me feel physically ill.

The spiritual work and mental reconditioning I'd done over the last decades prepared me to stay with this feeling in my chest, whatever it might be. Discomfort and mystery live side by side at the edge of growth. This particular combination, in this particular place, was just too valuable to ignore. Was something inside of me being hidden away or torn wide open? I was trying to ride through the experience without getting hung up on naming it.

Hungry as I could be for divine touch, I wanted to be guided to its meaning. At this point in my life, I hoped that I was finished with forcing revelation just to satisfy my princess ego. The queen surrenders into her relationship with Spirit and quits striving to feel uniquely and particularly blessed. The wise woman is ready to enter a new stage of humility, realizing that enlightenment isn't about "doing God better." Sovereign spirituality is about laying down the need to know, the need to be certain, and the need to rule.

And then, there was a rift in time. Suddenly, I was no longer a wise woman communing with my sister crow. I was no longer a queen who knew that the truest Sovereign is willing to kneel upon hallowed ground. Instead, I was a princess who had accidentally wandered into enemy territory. This place where my lovely, pious grandfather worshipped and found such solace in Jesus and his communion saints might look like a lovely sanctuary, but it was also a bastion of judgment.

We need to be willing to drop the spiritual armor and be vulnerable in order to reach the heavens above and true insights within. I've become good at practicing that and living that, but it wasn't safe to peel back the layers of my spirit in this place. There was too much human stuff mixed with the frankincense and myrrh. There were catacombs of shame that I never knew about, and they were ready to pull me in. This wasn't a spiritual experience. It was something more like a panic attack. *When did the Catholic Church last burn a book?* I plunged into a dark fantasy that my own book on women's personal, creative, and spiritual Sovereignty could stir up that kind of frenzy. The rebellious princess in me was rather excited by the prospect. Hasn't every good feminist wanted to write a banned book as proof that she was truly challenging the status quo? So much for my hard-earned humility and equanimity.

My wise woman tried to get my attention, reminding me that my work was more than an act of mere sedition. Even back in the day when I was fueled by defiant, wayward pagan grrrl power, I couldn't gather the energy to write a book out of pure spite. My Sovereign self knew that I was on a mission to heal and restore wholeness to a world splintered by all this divisive "us versus them" thinking. In that moment, as the deacon took to the pulpit to share his sermon, however, I couldn't remember that I'd reached this sensible conclusion. I was too busy worrying that this congregation would put down their hymnals and come after me like a mob. In the space of one religious service, I had gone from conferring with nature and a far-off bird to worrying that my unfinished book and I would be tossed onto a pyre like a medieval witch. In my growing hysteria, I also forgot that I rather *loved* the idea of being a medieval witch.

Amazing how the mere worry of what family and tribe might think can twist a fully grown woman into knots. I had become every inch the princess, all riddled with shadows and fears even more dramatic than those I conjured as a teenage apostate. There I was, quite sure that I was the center of the universe and that my paragraphs and pages might be enough to inspire a stampede. Caught up in this dark little romance, I wanted to be labeled a heretic as much as I wanted to be welcomed by the flock. Oh, the power our old wounds can have, especially when paired with a legacy of institutionalized stigma and shame. How intense the images a person can concoct within her own mind simply because she exercised her right to choose and then wandered back into the belly of the beast.

For a few agonizing minutes, I was ready to sacrifice at least one chapter of this book—or maybe the entire project altogether—so I could rework things and tell a simpler story that made women's Sovereignty seem like something that could be universally accepted and celebrated. *What in the hot and holy hell was I thinking?*

Just when I think I am standing at the center of my own intricate and well-designed Sovereignty Knot, I find myself spinning out of control. What sort of intergalactic wormhole did this family pew create in order to make me wonder if life could have been happier and easier if I had lived according to the code of clan? No longer gazing out the windows to the horizon, I got lost in the patterns of the cozy winter sweaters worn by all the praying people around me. In that moment, I considered writing my abortion right out of the story. I couldn't change the past—I didn't *want* to change the past—but I could edit it out for the sake of… what? My grandpa's devotion? My own devotion to my daughters' innocence? The opinions of those faceless strangers who would be offended by a clear-eyed, legal choice I made when I was twenty-five? I was ready to leave the chapter out of this book not because abortion is a deeply private, personal decision, but because standing in the midst of the so-called pro-life world almost convinced me that my reproductive destiny is not my own to control.

For a few minutes, the weight of this patriarchal body crushed me and I believed that my own body belonged to them. This wasn't all in my mind, of course. Even if Roe v. Wade has been the law of the land for nearly fifty years, the right to Sovereignty over your own skin is still not a foregone conclusion. At my first pro-choice march in Washington, D.C. in 2001, baby boomers carried signs saying "I can't believe we still have to protest this shit." You'll see the same women carrying the same signs today, especially since so many state legislatures attempted to ban the procedure in 2019. This sense of being attacked for my abortion and my support of abortion rights may have been the result of an overactive imagination in that moment, but the fear of persecution and prosecution are still terribly real for too many women.

This was a momentary bit of backsliding into shame and secrecy, but it still scares me. When I left the building twenty minutes later, I was already doing the internal repairs and breathing into the spaces that opened up in that miniature private breakdown. It's one of so many examples of how it's easy to speak of Sovereignty and celebrate a woman's independence, but it's quite another when you're faced with standing alone before the scrutiny—real or conjured—of family and the pressure of conservative belief.

I Don't Regret My Abortion

Here's the real truth that flooded back to me after I spent those desperate minutes wondering if should erase my own Sovereign feminist evolution in order to please the Catholic community: If I hadn't made that choice to terminate an unintentional pregnancy in 2004, my own little family would not be here today.

My husband and I met the old-fashioned way: in a bar. It would be great if the story was a simple "girl meets boy" scenario and a chance meeting turned into borrowing a pen from the bartender to scribble down a phone number so we could tell a story of our real first date a weekend later. In truth, simple doesn't interest me because simple never seems to happen to me. Our chance meeting turned into stumbling back to my place at 2AM. And that would turn into the next morning's sinking feeling of "What have I done...?" From the first instant we met, this man and I had a connection. That was proven in the dim light of dawn when we looked at each other, one of us a little foggy on the other's name, and knew we had just made something together. The morning-after pill wasn't available over the counter at that time. This was the dark ages when I had to dig up the phone book and turn to the Yellow Pages to find the number for a woman's health clinic. The midwife who answered the phone was waiting to hear from that weekend's pregnant moms. I must have sounded self-assured enough, and she must have seen the scenario unfold plenty of times. Without knowing any more than my name, she called in a prescription and I dealt with the massively magical hormonal assault that is taking a month's worth of birth control pills in one swallow.

The problem was: It didn't work.

Two weeks later when my reproductive system was supposed to be back to normal, I was calling Planned Parenthood for the kind of help they couldn't give over the phone. I needed three hundred dollars and a well-timed appointment so I could take an even more powerful pill called mifepristone, bleed heavily through the weekend, and get back to my new job at the library by Monday.

If I hadn't gotten pregnant, I bet I would have stopped seeing the guy who helped get me there. I was starved for independence, for art gallery openings, and weekend yoga retreats. I wanted to fall in love with myself, not some new man. When I'm being glib, I'd say I kept letting him call me and show up at my apartment unannounced because I needed cash to solve a problem. In reality, I had a credit card of my own. In reality, I didn't want to be alone through the experience. In reality, his obvious adoration was flattering. In reality, I truly enjoyed his company from the beginning. In reality, I needed to not be the chick who got knocked up after a one-night stand.

Never for a moment did I consider keeping the baby, though I did devote a great deal of myself to wondering if I should keep the man. Does this sound like the story of a callous, self-centered girl living an unexamined life? Honestly, it didn't ever feel that way. I was tuned into an understanding about who I was and what I was meant to do. A force that was so much greater than my fragile human agenda told me that this baby was never meant to be born into this world. "Little Soul," as I came to call her, was only ever meant to appear for a short time to perform one impossible task: cement the bond between Marisa and Mike so that, years later, Moira and Mairead could make their way into the world.

This is a choice that I couldn't bring myself to doubt, then or now. It was blessed and understood by every face of the divine I would care to direct my prayers toward. I've mourned Little Soul many times—especially after too much wine when all the unresolved feelings come in a wave of raw emotion—but even through my tears, I was more full of gratitude than regret. I'm grateful to live in an age when I have a choice. I'm grateful that my gamble on this man more than paid off. I'm grateful that I've found my way into a spirituality that allows me to feel like a connected and protected child of god rather than hopeless sinner. I'm grateful that Little Soul found her place amongst my goddesses and guides and is still their most powerful, palpable emissary. When I tune into that energy, I'm reminded that there is so much more at play than the exercise of my own will. Yes, I am grateful for my consciousness and my awakening, but I am even more grateful for the universal web of consciousness, the presence of a greater spirit that holds me and my humanity and helps me find my way.

I celebrate my wisdom, my receptivity, and my ability to trust myself enough to hear Little Soul's message. *I am only here to stay for a little while, but I have such great work to do. By letting me go, you're opening yourself to the great work you'll do when the time is right.*

If the work of the princess is to forgive herself for all the fuckups and shortcomings, I was at the height of my power when I was twenty-five. When I chose to move through that summer without guilt, self-hatred, and morning sickness, I surrendered into a real abiding love with the man Little Soul helped me choose. I got the chance to really fall for him, rather than feel yoked to him by shared custody or a too-soon marriage. This is the sort of individual Sovereign magic that ripples forth into the world and begins, ever so subtly, to change everything.

The Right to Choose and the Obligation to Tell the Whole Story

Having traveled so far during the space of this Mass without even rising for Communion, I returned my attention to the altar just as the priest began to address the latest scandal in the Church. The story hadn't become any less painful in its repetition as more clergy members were accused and convicted of sexual abuse.

There was a twist to this version because the now defrocked cardinal who covered up for the monsters was once bishop of this very diocese. Men who had violated the Sovereignty of children and other vulnerable people for decades loomed in the midst of these pious churchgoers and their own little kids. I'd feared these people would hate me for taking a pill that stopped something before it even really began. How could they possibly curse me for making my own legal and ethical choices when this kind of horror and deceit festered at the core of their organization? To think I nearly gave up telling a story that was so essential to my own Sovereignty and to this great trajectory of women's Sovereignty just to appear acceptable to a club I didn't even want to join.

To stand Sovereign in my life, I need to stand Sovereign in my stories. Sometimes, it's enough simply to remember what I felt and why I made the decisions I did. Some stories are never meant to be told on the public stage, but this one is different. A twenty-first century story of Sovereignty requires absolute honesty when it comes to sex and our ability to control its consequences. If I didn't tell my abortion story, if I let this sin of omission warp the narrative, I would be betraying all of us—me, my husband, our daughters, my feminist sisters, and even the true believers with their anti-choice bumper stickers and their obsession with praying the rosary for all of us fallen women. Women who have had abortions, both those who proudly tell their story and those who feel they must hide it like a dark secret, need to be reminded they are not alone. People who want to label women who have ended a pregnancy as hell-bound reprobates need to see the full humanity of someone who made a clear-eyed choice. Most importantly, Little Soul needs to be acknowledged as the most important person I never met.

Since there is no single road to Sovereignty, I understand that I could have decided to have that baby and I could have become a spectacular single mama who lived out any number of adventures. It's also possible that "you, me, and baby makes three" really could have worked way back then, but I think it would have been too much for our fragile new connection to bear. My future husband and I needed to fall in love on our own, and create a life together that had nothing to do with mutual obligation. Any of those possibilities are strange and foreign to me because they are not the life that I chose. That is not the life that chose me. I don't trust versions of the story that would have me betray my very first thought when I realized there was a possibility that I was pregnant: *I am not prepared to have this baby. This is not the time to become a mother.* My princess was scared and felt immeasurably stupid, but she was sure. My queen thought deeply about what it meant to create and offer care, but she was sure. My wise woman was already knitting a blanket, but as she tore out the stitches and rolled the yarn back into a ball, she was sure, too.

Now that I am a mother and I know what I gave up, do I regret the choice I made? No. I love my family too much to want to rewrite the reproductive story that made us the foursome we are today. I love my own spiritual path too much to pave over the past with stones borrowed from another faith mined in another time. I love the woman I have become too much to erase the chapters that wrote me into being.

Writing Prompt: A Woman's Right to Choose

As I said above, no story about twenty-first century women's Sovereignty would be complete without an exploration of sex and our ability to control its consequences. Take this opportunity to explore your own experiences when it comes to exercising your right to choose. Has your sexual and reproductive story been a story of Sovereignty?

Maybe it's time to tell your own abortion story through the lens of Sovereignty. Maybe this is an opportunity to wrangle with your own feelings about abortion, particularly your ambivalence. Maybe you found my story hard to swallow. Be honest about that and reckon with your own feelings about the way I exercised my own Sovereignty, because that's the surest way to learn about your relationship with your own.

CHAPTER 10

Embrace the Wise Woman

A young man falls in love with Truth and searches the wide world for her. He finds her in a small house, in a clearing, in a forest. She is old and stooped. He swears himself to her service—to chop wood, to carry water, to collect the root, the stem, the leaf, the flowering top, the seed of each plant she needs for her work.

Years go by. One day, the young man wakes up longing for a child. He goes to the old woman and asks to be released from his oath so that he may return to the world. *Certainly,* she says, *but on one condition: You must tell them that I am young and that I am beautiful.*

—*"Folktale"* by Paula Meehan[12]

---

12 Paula Meehan, *Pillow Talk* (Loughcrew, Ireland: Gallery Press, 1994), 50.

We're on a mission to ditch our misconceptions about age as we move in and out of our archetypes of princess, queen, and wise woman. It's my dream that everyone who reads this book will challenge the "old equals frail and incapable" paradigm and the "youth equals flaky and incapable" paradigm, too. It's my dream that we'll all encounter the changes in our bodies and our minds on our own terms, either surrendering or fighting back according to our own truths.

When you live according to Sovereign Time, you remember that chronological age isn't what determines your identity. All of the Sovereignty archetypes will empower you (and potentially hinder you) throughout life. Wisdom isn't tied to the date you were born or how many degrees you have. You gather wisdom when you're willing to be awake and receptive rather than distracted and numb.

When you stand Sovereign in your own being and your own health, you can challenge the artificially constructed beliefs about age that get made into flesh every day. Sheer positive thinking can't keep your organs functioning the same way at eighty as they did at twenty, but neither do you have to accept the story that says every decade comes with a new host of problems. Is menstruation really a curse that only gets worse with the years? Does getting older mean that you must walk with a slow, hesitant shuffle? Is it inevitable that someday you'll be too old to give and receive sensual pleasure? There are certain immutable realities that come with being embodied over time, but you don't have to follow the regular schedule of physical decline.

Body Sovereignty isn't a topic that we have space to explore fully in this book, but I invite you to think about how you can apply these ideas to the way you see and treat your own body each day. When you visit a doctor or read an article about preventing a disease, are you standing in your Sovereignty? We need experts, research, and treatments that extend and improve lives, but there's a lot of paranoia and profit-driven advice out there, too. The time when you most need self-trust and a strong sense of agency is when sitting in an exam room, but, unfortunately, a paper smock that exposes your ass is the opposite of a Sovereign's gown. In such moments when you feel vulnerable and just plain *old*, the princess is there to keep you supple and the queen is there to remind you that you're strong. The wise woman is there to illuminate every step of the way, whether you're waiting for medical test results or setting off on a solo hike when most of your friends are worried about hip replacements.

Body Sovereignty isn't all about life and death either. The conversations with my hair stylist about whether it's time to hide the fresh strands of silver feel more existential than cosmetic. Do I want to start coloring my hair in search of that more vibrant red that would make me (almost) feel twenty again? Or do I want to hold onto my "unicorn hairs" that my daughters count with such loving attention? Each white streak represents a sorrow or a stress I survived, after all. The salon can be a battleground for Sovereignty and personal truth. It's the place where you decide how you want to change, preserve, and present your body. It's also where you must reckon with your motivations. Does the decision to dye your hair come from an authentic desire to try something new, reclaim something you loved, or the fear that you won't be accepted if you don't look the way you used to?

For now, I'm sticking with color that four decades of living has made, a sort of muted red-gold that only hints at the rich fire that

I still consider my "real" hair. There's a comfort in knowing the shade of my youth is only a few semi-toxic chemicals away should I decide I want it back. The slackening skin of my neck and the puffy patches under my eyes, on the other hand... Sometimes I'm startled to see that tired-looking woman in the mirror, the one who will never get the sleep required to recover the way her eyes are *supposed* to look when she smiles. But then, just like the desire to erase the painful, complicated chapters of my life that wrote me into being, my desire to erase the evidence of the years from my body is a fleeting one. I don't always love the way that exhaustion and worry have been etched into my skin, but I do love who I can be when I quit worrying about whether I need to book a laser treatment. When I give myself permission to inhabit a reality that's grounded in more than the firm, unlined rules of beauty, I can be free to fully inhabit all the spirals of my being, wrinkles, dimples, saggy bits, stretch marks, and all. When I can see myself in the mirror as I am, not as a faded copy of who I used to be, I begin to see like a wise woman.

The Cailleach in the Mirror

In the Irish and Scottish world, the old woman, the holy hag, the wisest of the wise is called the Cailleach. Not to be confused with the death crone, this great lady is recognized as a profound creative force. She is the healer. She mediates our relationship with the otherworld. The Cailleach is an entire galaxy of myth unto herself, but many of her stories take us to the heart of Sovereignty. In later stories, she mixes with mortal men as many of her shapeshifting Sovereign sisters do, but in the oldest tales the Cailleach birthed and shaped the landscape itself. The stones themselves are her bones. Many look to the Cailleach as the goddess of the goddesses, the one who came before those younger deities we might know, like Brigid and the Morrígan. Though I've loved the *idea* of the Cailleach ever since I started playing in these misty fields of Celtic spirituality, she only just started to become *real*.

Storytellers have a way of reaching across time and space and making concepts into characters who can change lives. I have the good fortune of knowing one such storyteller well. Elizabeth Cunningham is the author and poet who gave the world The Maeve Chronicles, novels that invite you to believe that Mary Magdalen was a fiery-haired Celt from the mythical Island of Women, *Tír na mBan*. The Cailleach lives on this island, too, and plays a vital role in the heroine Maeve's becoming. It takes a wise woman to know a wise woman, and Elizabeth can write a wise woman—a *bean feasa*, if you want to be able to say it in the Irish—like no one I have ever read.

Elizabeth isn't just one of my favorite writers, she is also one of my most trusted advisors. Every few weeks, we sit down together and discuss my search for Sovereignty. This book of mine has been my mirror, and it was becoming clear that I couldn't complete it until I figured out how to make the wise woman into someone not just woven of myth, but part of my own reality. With Elizabeth's gentle guidance, I met the facet of the Cailleach I was ready to know: my sixty-year-old self. Actually, this future version of me was twenty-seven days past her sixtieth birthday. She—*I*—was exactly one day older than my mother was on the day she died, and it was clear that this dream-woman had every intention of welcoming many more decades of wisdom into her life. This older, wiser woman wore my face, though the angles had changed as flesh surrendered to gravity. The vague creases around the eyes had turned into a network of canyons and crags. I like to think those lines will come from all the laughing and reading I'll do over the next twenty years.

The life that my future self leads is a good one. Offering me a cup of tea beneath the shade of a gnarled grandmother tree that shelters a white cottage nestled into an Irish hill, she tells me this is her home. She tells me this is *my* home. The wise woman reminds me over and over that she is *me* and that this vision is as real as any memory that emerges when we're riding time in the Sovereignty Knot. All that I have been and all that I'll get to be over my century on this earth are sheltered there under that great tree. A version of me at every age and every stage dwells in her heartwood.

My future self and I speak as wise women do, covering essential topics like the exact flavor of Irish sunshine, the importance of slathering on extra sunscreen on your brow and extra butter on scones, and how the most common metaphors are often the most true. "This is our Tree of Life," she says, gesturing to the boughs that arch overhead. "Within his tree," she explains, "flows the golden current that is the universal love of creation, the life force that rushes within all of us." I nod, knowing that she has found a clearer way to express something I have always known.

This kind of clarity is brilliant and enchanting, and absolutely terrifying. Our own inherent power flows within us, as silent and invisible as sap in a tree. At the same time, our power is just so *big*, a force of nature that's too fast and too strong to be held within the fragile human psyche. But the wise woman, who is falsely accused of fragility all too often, knows that we're all capable of containing and channeling the dizzying flood of energy within.

I've been carrying a line from novelist Jeanette Winterson in my heart since I was twenty years old: "I don't want to eke out my life like a resource in short supply. The only selfish life is a timid one. To hold back, to withdraw, to keep the best in reserve, both overvalues the self, and undervalues what the self is."[13] In this moment with my future-tense self, I could finally be with the abundance of life, and see how it's always available to the individual as well as the collective. All I needed to do was release my great lingering fear: My life would be as short as my mom's. My older, wiser self invited me to take her hand and give myself fully to the gold, to life, to Sovereignty. To be afraid of the liquid gold of Sovereignty is to be afraid to *live*. I do not want to be afraid to live anymore—even if the world can be confusing, uncertain, and cruel. Regret, fear, grief, and pain may loom large, but they can never totally subsume that golden tide that moves within us all.

A Cailleach Story

In the years since my mother's death, I have had to reacquaint myself with the possibility—and the hope—that I will have the opportunity to grow old. In *If Women Rose Rooted*, Sharon Blackie discusses what's possible as we age and she makes the latter part of life sound extraordinary:

> To a woman of the Celtic nations, to become Elder is above all to become Cailleach: to represent the integrity

---

13 Jeanette Winterson, *The PowerBook* (New York: Alfred A. Knopf, 2001), 203.

and the health of the wild places and creatures of the world. To become Elder is to become strong—strong as the white old bones of the earth, strong enough to endure the long, lonely vigil to the end of the world. Above all, to become Elder is to become the *bean feasa*, the Wise Woman: the one who knows the secrets and speaks the languages of the land, who speaks with the moral authority of the Otherworld, who weaves the dreaming of the world.[14]

I know I'm ready…

I have long searched out stories of the Cailleach that speak to my heart. There are times when you wait for the goddesses and the guides to find you, and there are times when you go out in search of them, courting meaning. On my quest for the Cailleach, I gathered morsels of story from here and let them marinate within my own spiritual imagination. When these stories resonated with elements from my own history and my own emotional needs, the Cailleach could take shape in my inner world. This particular story is inspired by and adapted from Gearóid Ó Crualaoich's important collection of folklore and analysis, *The Book of the Cailleach*.

Fádo fádo…

There once lived an old, old woman they called An Chailleach Bhéarthach *whose bare feet seemed to never stop moving across the land. She was a strange thing to be sure, and people said she never shed a tear, never cooked a meal, and lived upon cow's milk alone.*

---

14 Sharon Blackie, *If Women Rose Rooted* (Tewkesbury, England: September Publishing, 2016), 308-309.

Perhaps she was treading magic into the land or perhaps she took the magic of the land into herself with each step. Whatever the reason, she was uncommonly careful to rinse the mud and the mire from her feet and legs whenever she walked through a boggy place.

There came a day when she crossed the doorsill of a church for the first time. Something in the priests' holy place spoke to her wild soul and she began to attend Mass every Sunday. Creature of the earth that she was, she always picked up a stone on her way home from the church. After years of Sundays, she had enough stones to fill a chest that was big enough to bury her in.

One day, a neighbor woman called out to her. "I hear that congratulations are in order! A new daughter in your line. How lovely…"

The Cailleach nodded her thanks and hurried on to her daughter's house, for she had not heard the happy news. "Daughter of mine!" she cried when she reached her daughter's cottage. The woman who appeared at the door looked like the great-grandmother she was. "Mother! What news?"

Though she'd traveled over the spine of the mountains and leapt over the lap of the river to make the call, the Cailleach wasn't a bit out of breath. "Your daughter's daughter gave birth to a daughter last night!" Never one to slow her pace, the Cailleach departed immediately, making a great loop over to the cliffs that loomed high above the sea and continuing on until she was back to the snug cave she called her home.

A hundred years later, the Cailleach had welcomed many more daughters to her hallowed bloodline. Moving a little bit more slowly than she had the century before, she took more time for gentle conversation. When an old man who was nearly as wizened and gray as the Cailleach herself appeared in the clearing by her cave, she bid him welcome. Figuring her visitor would be impressed that an otherworldly creature such as she would take the time to observe the rituals of the Church, she pointed out her great chest of stones. She told him that it was quite full, a clear sign of her weekly devotion.

"Is that so?" asked the old man. He seemed such an agreeable sort, so she didn't refuse him when he asked to look inside to see her blessed hoard. When they lifted the lid there were but two small pebbles huddled at the bottom of that great box. The Cailleach was puzzled to see it empty, but one wouldn't say she was embarrassed or too greatly chagrined.

The kind man remarked gently, "Ah well, simple enough. It seems you only truly heard the Mass twice in all your comings and goings across the years." He gathered his cane and hat and set out again, saying over his shoulder as he picked his way down the path that led from the cave, "You're a good woman, all the same!"

Some say that the man was a messenger from the Christian God, there to lay gentle claim to a mostly pagan soul. Some say that she shed the first tears in her long life when she realized that the magic of only two Masses took root within her over all those years of Sundays. Then there are others who might ask how anyone could know if tears fell on her cheeks.

Who can know the full story of a woman who could walk the spine of a mountain range in the space of a morning and cross the lap of a river in one great leap? How can anyone truly know a woman content to live alone in a snug cave at the end of the world?

When I started seeking out Cailleach stories, I immediately dismissed any that hinted at her conversion or described her outright elimination at the hands of the Church. I was channeling the same impulse that caused me to ignore stories of Saint Brigid when I was a young scholar in search of the Goddess. My mission is to reclaim the divine feminine from all those patriarchal incursions, not sit idly by and read about how she was subsumed. As I look at my story and my own experiences with religion and spirituality, however, I'm less likely to dismiss the tales that blend the Christian with the pagan. My experience in that New Jersey church taught me that the institution still has a hold on me. That's something to notice and resist, particularly since it has the potential to send me into a cyclone of doubt and shame, but there's more to my connection with Christianity than a legacy of repression. Stories like this one that describe how the Goddess herself made peace with the new religion but still could not be fully tamed have significance for me. This eclectic spirituality of mine may be sourced from the spirals of divine feminine presence I find in the natural world, but it's built on a foundation created by generation upon generation of Catholicism. The wise woman in me knows that the way to wholeness and integration and, ultimately, Sovereignty, is to recognize all aspects of the self. Christianity is an essential aspect of Irish culture and my own family culture. It's not my path, but I can only benefit from acknowledging that I am always going to be in relationship with the Church, just as the Cailleach was in this story. I'll never get everything I need from the Mass, but I can still follow my nanna's advice: A quick Hail Mary always helps.

Meet Your Wise Woman

The wise woman is the seer of all that is. Light and dark, youth and age, kindness and cruelty, reminding us that one has never existed without the other. She is the tender of the cauldron that holds the seen and unseen, the comfortable and all that seems too hard to bear. She is the keeper of all knowledge, though she's apt to lose track of language as soon as she gets the spell just right. She is the gentle grandmother, and the fierce hag in the hut at the end of the lane. She is the one who helps us hold the most difficult truths: This world is gorgeous and terrible, and we are destined to live only until we die. The wise woman within us is here to do the most difficult, necessary work, making us aware of the place before birth and the place beyond death, even as we lose ourselves in the distractions of every living day.

The wise woman exists in each of us, even when we try to deny her, even if we say we want nothing to do with her talk of mortality and eternity. She understands that our fear renders her mute and invisible. She knows we don't necessarily fear the body itself, but we're bloody afraid of its inevitable failure and that, someday, we won't be able to flow, to fuck, to fool around. (She protects our tender hearts, and she also tells it like it is. When you tend the liminal spaces between everything we know in this life and the great unnameable unknown, you need poetry, profanity, and silence in equal measure.)

The wise woman is Truth, but that's not a simple title to hold in our complex, ambiguous, ever-changing world. She is beautiful, but she does not wear the face of beauty we have been taught to crave and adore. She is youth, but only when you compare her to the universe that was created before clocks. She takes tea with the ancients and wanders within the dreams of the gods.

We are called to set a place for the wise woman. We need to stand in her presence and ask her to be present within us so that we can be fully awake to all the wonder that needs to be witnessed and all the wounds that need to be healed. We must prepare ourselves to do the wise woman's magic and remember that we *can* change our consciousness according to our will. She is the one who helps us meet and surrender to the inevitable changes in our cells, the sorrow that comes with death, and the loss that comes with time. She teaches us that surrender is not powerlessness and does not need to feel like defeat. She holds us as we bear witness to the relentless blend of joy and suffering that tugs us from cradle to grave.

I have seen flashes of the wise woman within myself throughout my life. Everyone who follows some mysterious, subterranean sense of "I just know" has been touched by her hand. The wise woman nudged me toward feminism, myth, and new spiritual frontiers when I was still in my teens. She pushed me to start studying Reiki and energy medicine before I even finished college. She led me to teachers, mentors, and sacred places that felt like coming home. The wise woman must have been present the night I met my husband, whispering that it was safe to trust this man. She took the tiller of my tiny boat and sailed me over the sea of grief and made sure I landed on the other side. She carried me through the most impossible moments of labor and helped me through those interminable nights with a newborn when I thought I was too depleted to stitch together one more shred of mother love.

The wise woman works through me when I offer hands-on or intuitive healing to others. She holds the great cauldron of human compassion so I can hold stories and confidences. When I am fully in my wise woman self, I can discern when people simply need to be heard, when they need to be healed, and when they need help shaping their story into a form that will inspire others. When I am at my best—when I am most authentic, Sovereign, and free—the wise woman is lighting me from within. And yet, it's often difficult to trust and access her power. Part of becoming wise is to come to understand why you resist being a keeper of wisdom.

With the embrace of the wise woman comes her gifts: spirituality, equanimity, acceptance, stillness, divine surrender, insight, humor, irreverence, renewal, alchemy, completion, and wholeness. Wouldn't we all want that? Wouldn't we all want access to the golden light that lovingly burns away all the shadows of self-doubt and self-loathing? Wouldn't we all want to experience the sense of divine connection to nature and the essence of creation? Yes, but no. We all have our reasons for closing our minds and hearts to her, for choosing to stay in struggle and deciding we need to sort it out all on our own. We often cannot embrace the wise woman's transformative magic because we are caught in her own unhealthy patterns: depression, isolation, passivity, stagnation, spiritual bypassing, and fear of change.

Our excuses are probably as profound as they are flimsy. I have been afraid to step fully into my wise woman self because I am afraid my life will be too short for me to do things properly. When I see that idea on the page, I recognize it's a limiting belief based on all sorts of flawed logic and residual grief. Thank the goddess for the wise woman within and the wise women in my circle who support me and who have the patience and presence to help me untangle the truth.

The Wise Woman Considers Mortality

The Cailleach is not associated with death, but another wise, Sovereign Irish fairy woman is. The Banshee is known by her wail, what's called a *caoin* in the Irish. She is the one who taught Irishwomen to mourn and raise a keening song. It is not her job to bring comfort. She is merely the messenger, delivering the news that is the only thing as sure as birth: death.

In this conversation about fully inhabiting life, about recognizing the rush of gold at the heart of creation, why would we want to open ourselves to the Banshee's song? As it turns out, listening to the call of death may be the greatest gift you can offer your wild, passionately alive self. As the Dalai Lama says, "Analysis of death is not for the sake of becoming fearful but to appreciate this precious lifetime."[15]

Maybe you're someone who lingers on the issue of mortality from time to time. Perhaps you've been told that you consider your own death more often than others consider "healthy." And maybe you're someone who likes to stay in the "good vibes only" terrain and see these ideas as a drag on the spirit. Let your wise woman hold you, wherever you are along that spectrum. Let her bring you back to the gold if you sink too deep and consideration becomes morbidity. Let her draw you into the cave if you're too dedicated to the light to consider the shadows.

---

15 His Holiness the Dalai Lama, *Mind of Clear Light: Advice on Dying and Living a Better Life* (New York: Atria Books, 2003), 39.

Writing Prompt: Mortality

Explore your feelings around your own certain fate: dying and leaving this life.

So much grief will flow when you think of everyone who has passed on before you and everyone you think you cannot live without. For now, ease aside your feelings about the deaths of others, both those you've endured and those you imagine.

Focus on yourself here—be truly Sovereign and stand as witness to your own thoughts, beliefs, projections, and fear. Consider your own fears, worry, and wonder about your own eventual passage into death.

Trust that the wise woman within you knows more about mortality and the spaces between than your conscious mind has ever explored. Trust her to hold you as you write into your life's relationship with death.

The Wise Woman Considers Eternity

On the other side of our fear of mortality, there's a whole other realm of possibility: eternity. You may have a vision of heaven that makes eternity feel quite real, but for those of us who do not, it can feel like there's a void at the other side of the known world that is too vast to contemplate. That which we feel we cannot understand can become a breeding ground for fear. Sovereignty depends on an eyes-wide-open relationship with reality, including the things that scare us about the great Unknown. What if you could release those fears and, instead, begin to wrap your mind around a fresh infinity that exists beyond everything we've been taught to see and touch?

These matters of mortality and eternity are questions that roll about in the silence of the mind, but remember that the path of healing and Sovereignty is never meant to be a solitary one. Get help from a trusted friend or counselor when you find you're struggling to wrap your mind around these impossible questions. Your wise woman has a cave of her own, but she always remembers and relies upon the power of community and sisterhood.

Writing Prompt: Eternity

What do you believe happens when we die?

Your exploration of mortality (in the prompt above) is the place to entertain the human sadness, fear, and worry that is attached to death. Use this writing prompt to wonder about the nature of eternity and what might exist on the other side of the veil. Use this prompt to entertain infinite possibility.

If your theology offers some clear insights into this question, take some time to put them on the page and then explore your feelings around these teachings. If your faith doesn't offer a vision of the afterlife, or if you don't engage with a spirituality that gives such guidance, dive into your own beliefs and questions.

The Territory of the Wise Woman

The princess plays on the cliffs. The queen creates her own castle. The wise woman's realm is in the cave. I've already taken you to Oweynagat, to the cave where the wise woman slipped into my heart. Even when you enter that cave with companions, the journey is into yourself. Not every cave is about being alone, however. There's another cave that exists in my imaginal world that my spirit visits all the time, and it's a place to be in community. I invite you to join with the wise women who sit in counsel in the most secret of all caves, at their home in the belly of the earth.

You are entering the realm of the wise women. This is their collective, their hive, their nest, their laboratory, their concert hall. This is the place where the drummers gather. Here, they sustain the pulse of life, the constant thrum of the planetary heart that echoes in the beat of every animal heart.

They are sitting in counsel. There are twelve women in this circle. In the flickering firelight, they are old, they are young, they are ageless. Their complexions reflect the earth herself—deepest dark of rich soil, the lush red of clay, the pale glow of sand. They are the world. You are in the belly of the Mother.

You have been expected. You are here to become the thirteenth sister, the thirteenth moon, the thirteenth womb. You are the catalyst for transformation. You are peace and surrender. You are wild knowing and sacred understanding. You are the anarchic laughter of a fabulous creature who has seen it all.

Where do you need to sit? In the midst of the circle? There is a sacred pool there and you are welcome to come to soak in their healing. You are welcome to be the wise woman who has deep needs, who needs her cup to be filled again.

Or, are you called to join the circle and take a drum? Do you have a song to sing to them? Are you feeling strong and ready to be heard? Perhaps so emboldened by these wise sisters, you realize you have a prophecy to share. Maybe you wish to invite your sisters to dance with you, dervishes with drums, ecstatically beating out a new song.

Take your place. Know you can return here and take another position in the circle at any time. This place is always open to you. You are always at home here. You are called to arrive and depart from this womb in the core of the earth whenever you need healing and community. In this place, you know you are part of the heartbeat, the song of the universe itself.

Keep receiving. Keep drumming. Keep singing. Keep dancing. Let part of your soul stay here always so you know how to come back...

Writing Prompt: The Cave and Your Wise Woman

Give yourself the time and space to fully describe your journey into the belly of the earth.

What did you need when you arrived in that circle of women? What did you see, smell, taste, hear, and feel? How were your needs satisfied? What do you imagine you might need and offer the next time you join them in their ecstatic drumming, dance, and song?

CHAPTER 11

On Running Over a Snake

It was a rainy September morning. Far south, a hurricane was spinning madly and we were experiencing the far fringes of that deadly storm. A thousand miles away, lives were being torn apart, but it only cost us the time it took to find galoshes as we splashed our way into a typical Tuesday. Driving my little one to preschool, I was operating at the usual level of preoccupation. For all my fascination with ancient wisdom, I've long been a current events addict. The reality TV politics that has whipped America into a frenzy since 2016 has only made my obsession worse, but recently I had been trying to ease back on my media diet. My mind had been clearer, and my thoughts had felt more like my own since I removed the Twitter app from my phone. Less of a victim of the latest communal outrage, I was beginning to shape

209 ☖

the narrative inside my own head. There was a chance I could have been more aware of the natural world as it unfolded around me, but I squandered that magic when I turned on the radio to get the national headlines. Talk of sexual assault and the latest Supreme Court nominee drew me right back into old patterns of incoherent anger and helplessness. Being a conscious, informed citizen of the world was necessary, but it has its price.

On this particular morning, a long black snake paid that price.

Maybe it wasn't just the newscast. Blame the rain. Blame the dawdling kid and my grumbling empty stomach. Blame my endless to-do list and my chronic fear that there was never enough time. Blame the whole modern world that seems to be designed to mute all of our senses except those that send us into the stratosphere of fury, the chasm of despair, and the dullness of consumption. If you want, you can blame the three-ton SUV, the reliance on gas-guzzling vehicles, or the Eisenhower administration's big bet on the U.S. highway system. Propelled by the weight of history and my own host of worries, I simply didn't have time to stop for anything so small and insignificant as a reptile that couldn't even be bothered to grow feet.

I'd tell you I want justice at the individual and the global scale, for humans, animals, and the earth, but I was just as unseeing as that blindfolded Greek goddess who holds the scales of justice as I barreled down that country road. My allegiance to contemporary distraction rendered the natural world invisible. It's easy to wish for equality and justice, and it's almost as easy to speak and write about them from behind the comfort of a computer screen. But then, it's not so easy to put these ideals into practice.

The affairs in my head were in all sorts of disarray as I sped along with barely a care for wildlife or anything else that wasn't directly related to my own competing priorities. If there's anything to this whole idea that humans are here to act as good stewards of the earth, I was failing at the job. Damn Mother Nature and her children. Bring on the speed, the senseless endangerment, and the accidental cruelty. Huh... Maybe I wasn't so different than those newsmakers and world shakers who made my blood boil with their narcissism and naked ambition.

There was a lesson in power and influence here, just waiting to be learned. As is so often the way, someone or something had to be sacrificed in the teaching. Whether we want to or not, we are constantly enacting the broken story of power, exerting our will over others just because we can. Everyone else who is winning in this system seems to be doing it, why not me? I'm in the habit of being the unheeding, reckless conqueror because I simply have more heft and horsepower behind me. My inherited privilege and prestige as an educated white woman with enough wealth for a car, a preschool tuition, and a house with more bathrooms than I ever have time to clean prepares me to exert all sorts of unconscious power. Sometimes, I take it out on an animal in the streets because slowing down would be inconvenient. Mostly, it's about senselessly consuming resources and staying comfy at the expense of the underpaid people who make my clothes and pick my food.

Let's get back to the defenseless animal that got me thinking about all this. (I'm nearly positive it was nonvenomous, but even if she were, no snake deserves to be run down by a set of all-weather tires.) The snake is a symbol of the goddess the world over, representing regeneration and rebirth, cycles of renewal, cycles of the earth, and the cycles of the body itself. Magical from the start, the snake held particular power for the ancient Egyptians and Greeks, as well as the medieval European alchemists who followed. The alchemists—both scientists and magicians in one—drew the *ouroboros*, the symbol of the snake swallowing her tail, to represent infinity and wholeness. This magic endures, particularly in a woman's life, marked as it is by so many twists and turns. The trinity knot that we use to represent Sovereignty might just be a holy serpent, calling us into an intricate dance through life.

That very morning, my older daughter had been asking about the story of Adam and Eve as we waited for her school bus. I did my best to stick to the Genesis version of the story, but I also gave her the feminist take that "Eve was framed." I left the door open to the idea that maybe the serpent who offered the knowledge of good and evil wasn't such a bad fellow after all.

Come to think of it, I've long been on the side of the snake. You know the one about Saint Patrick driving the serpents out of Ireland, of course. Nice yarn, that one. Thing is, there hadn't been any snakes on the island since at least the last ice age. Herpetology and geology aside, in the metaphorical realm where this stuff really matters, St. P. was credited with striking the first blow against paganism, bringing the new Christian faith that would all but eliminate the old beliefs that were native to that land. He was there to raise his crozier against Mother Ireland and her people's serpentine faith that looped round and round with the endless cycles of the seasons. He was there to change history and create the Ireland we know today. He was also there to lay the foundations of a particular kind of patriarchal dominance that would hold the country in thrall for well over 1,500 years.

Saint Patrick and his missionary friends came to Ireland and changed the story that people had been living for millennia. They weren't the first guys, nor were they the last, to destroy a sacred feminine image and use it for their own purposes.

And I had just ground a snake into the pavement of Loughlan Lane.

Two Sovereignty Goddesses and a Hero

Fadó fadó…

Five royal brothers were out hunting in the wildest, most remote part of Ireland. The stag they chased took them deeper into the wilderness than they'd ever been before and, as night fell and they sought shelter in the forest, they had neither food nor water.

Oh, but what luck! They came across a well. But, just as the eldest brother was about to reach down and take a drink, a loathsome hag appeared. Hairy chin, pocked face, milky eye… the full nightmare of the aging feminine stood before them.

"I am the guardian of this sacred well," she announced. "You can drink all that you like, but you must kiss me first."

This particular young man was accustomed to the pretty young things who hung about the castle. He'd rather die of thirst than give himself to such a wizened crone. He told her so and went off to sulk and lick his own dry lips.

Picture a similar scene with the next three brothers. Thirsty, arrogant lads and an old woman who stands her ground, wrapped not in an embrace, but in a lonely passion for her work as protector of the sacred well. Youthful stubbornness and ancient dedication, side by side.

But then, the youngest brother, Niall, came forward. For the fifth time, the guardian makes her offer, "You can drink all that you like, but you must kiss me first."

He kissed her. The old woman was transformed into a siren who would give any modern fantasy heroine a run for her money, and the two didn't stop when they hit first base. He had met the Sovereignty Goddess and she found him worthy. Not too long after, thanks to her aid, Niall would become King of all Ireland and this magical being from the well would be his queen.

Cynics may say that Niall was just terribly parched. Romantics may say he saw something in that elder's eye. Students of myth may say that he'd heard this one before and knew that there was more than a tumbler of water in his future if he accepted her offer. Feminists read it differently still, but we will get to that in a moment.

The old woman, of course, was a Sovereignty Goddess in disguise. Not only is she the keeper of sacred waters and a protector of natural resources, but she embodies the sanctity of the earth as well. As fits the model of the myths, the Sovereignty Goddess bestows kingship on the man who is worthy of her, the land, and the people who live upon it. For at least part of the story, she's the real force behind the throne.

So, that's all just lovely, right? I was pleased enough with the compact grace of the tale and told it that way for years. It had all the necessary elements, including the wise woman shapeshifter and the one guy who could escape toxic masculinity and ageism to see the potential beneath the sagging skin. Everything went according to plan as the goddess found her match and the country got a just ruler who would care for its resources and its populace. Sure, the Sovereignty Goddess drops out of the story after her boy makes it to the big time and she doesn't actually seem to have a name, but it's a story that *works*.

Then I did what the wise woman does: I kept reading beyond the first page of search results. Giving myself permission to go deeper, to dive beneath that which I thought I knew well. Thanks to analysis by writers like Gearóid Ó Crualaoich in *The Book of the Cailleach*, I saw that I was barely scratching the surface of my understanding of this particular tale. There was another goddess standing in plain sight, but I never bothered to get to know her story in my rush to share the simple narrative. For the sake of convenience, I'd been leaving out essential details that are actually the most important of all. This is how I *should* have been telling it all along…

Fadó fadó, the king of Ireland's sons entered the forest for a long hunt.

Four of the brothers always walked first—Brian, Ailill, Fiachra, and Fergus. These were the sons of Queen Mongfionn, the Sacred Queen. The youngest brother, Niall, always came last. He was not the son of Mongfionn but of Caireann, the daughter of an English king. No doubt Niall was instructed to take his place last in line, for Mongfionn hated him and had long since cursed him with her sorcery. He was the son of a woman who seduced her husband, after all. More than that, he was the son of a people who would invade her beloved Ireland.

There was a poet by the name of Torna, however, who took pity on the boy, sheltering him when he could. Torna put forth a prophecy that Niall—not one of his legitimate, well-born brothers—would one day hold the kingship. In fact, the poet declared, Niall's descendants, the Uí Néills would rule Ireland forever.

The story goes on just as the first version did. The thirsty lads encountered the keeper of well, and that was followed by the kissing, the shapeshifting, and the king-making. As I used to tell it, the focus is purely on the old hag turned fresh young Sovereignty Goddess; the boys' mothers don't factor in at all. But here's the thing: The back story really matters. Bear with me for just a moment as we dive into the intricacies of Irish mythology. The political intrigue of ancient kingdoms doesn't have any particular bearing on how we live out our Sovereignty today, but there's a great deal to learn from the way the winners rewrote history.

Since the princes' father, King Eochaid, was the rightful king of all Ireland, that means that the Sovereignty Goddess would have chosen him to take the throne back when he was a young man. His was still married to that same Sovereignty Goddess years later. The tale that got passed through history doesn't mention that Mongfionn is a Sovereignty Goddess, however. Instead, Mongfionn, who Ó Crualaoich associates with meaning "Sacred Queen,"[16] is said to be a sorceress who curses her husband's bastard son.

---

16 Gearoid Ó Crualaoich. *The Book of the Cailleach* (Cork: Cork University Press, 2003), 42.

Why wouldn't one of Eochaid and Mongfionn's four legitimate sons inherit the throne? The storytellers give us a reason: None of those brash young men were noble enough to embrace the hag. As I said, for years I accepted this meaning as a neat and simple example of the shapeshifting Sovereignty Goddess choosing a worthy king, but something stinks about this story. You know why? The Sovereignty Goddess who chose Niall to become king did not have a name.

Niall would end up heading a dynasty, and the Uí Néill family would wield power in Ireland for generations. In order to legitimize that power, the people surrounding Niall and his descendants would create a divine sort of pedigree for their founding father. They cast the real Sovereignty Goddess, Mongfionn, as a vindictive woman scorned, and they invented a nameless new cardboard cutout goddess in order to justify their spurious claim to the throne.

Why am I going to all these lengths to get you to understand the political calculations in a story that's well over a thousand years old? Because every time we turn on the news someone is trying to spin the truth to suit their own purposes and benefit their own party. The story of women's power has been corrupted, co-opted, and twisted across the millennia, just as it is now in everyday life. It happens on the political stage and it happens to us all. We know that the girl on the playground, the princess in all her boisterous glory, will be prettified and told she's too loud. We know that woman at the head of the table, the queen in all her confident savvy, will be vilified and told she's a bitch. We know that the elder who still plays the game of life, the wise woman in all her venerable experience, will be disrespected and told she's too slow.

We're on a mission to reclaim our feminine power and the magic. The story of Mongfionn and her unnamed replacement is a blueprint for how such treasures can be stolen away. We're reviving and reshaping the concept of Sovereignty in order to counter an ancient legacy of collective repression and countless incidents of individual abuse. In our modern political culture of lies, cover-ups, and distortions, it's never been more important to think about who controls the narrative and what, if anything, we can accept at face value. When we can spot one instance in which a story was co-opted or manufactured to preserve one group's authority and control, we can start to do it in other stories, with the latest headlines, and in our own experiences. We can use these skills every time we're called to speak truth to power, but particularly when we're talking about the fate of oppressed people and the state of the environment. Despite what the bullies in the legislatures and the executive offices might try to pull over on us, we'll be able to look deeper.

Before we leave Mongfionn and get back to the events of the day, do something for me. Please remember her name. It's tough to pronounce and even if you are saying it right it's not necessarily beautiful to the non-Irish speaker, but it needs to be remembered. When a character in a myth has a name, it means they're important. Then, as now, both to possess and to give a name is a sign of great power. When we can see the families at America's southern border as people with names and individual identities, and not just a faceless hoard causing an immigration crisis, we find the power to create humane policies. When we can see entire villages displaced by rising seas and desertification as people with individual identities, and not just waves of climate refugees crowding someone else's cities, we find the will to solve both the climate crisis and the humanitarian crisis.

The quest for Sovereignty on our own terms asks us to craft alternative versions of the oppressive stories we've been taught to believe. Recognize the power you have—and often squander—when it comes to holding and focusing your own attention. Allow yourself to see how your attention has been conquered and occupied, either by modern marketers and politicians or by storytellers who speak for so-called tradition and place a singular claim on the truth. Mistress of your own attention, you become Sovereign in your own mind and in your own living story. You then gather the power to change the narrative so we treat all people and animals as they should be treated, here on a planet that truly can sustain all the life that grows upon it right now.

Sovereignty: Personal, Political, Ecological

In the end, I was given a great gift. When I drove over that same patch of road twenty minutes later, slowly this time both because it was raining harder and because I knew I would have to come face-to-face with my cruelty, the snake was gone. I can allow myself to imagine that I only clipped her tail and didn't damage any vital organs. It's nice to believe that snakes are unimaginably strong. Perhaps there was some reptile-loving pedestrian with a predilection for downpours who saved the beast and took it home to heal—or at least gently moved it to the side of the road. Wouldn't it be lovely to think there was some sort of miracle at play and that the Goddess herself heard my heartfelt prayers of remorse and came to the creature's aid? No matter what, I was not faced with my mistake a second time. I feel grateful, though perhaps a bit unworthy of being spared my share of guilt.

To declare yourself a seeker of Sovereignty is to dedicate yourself to ending the cycles of abuse and neglect we humans have inflicted upon the land since commerce and technology disrupted our relationship with the soil. Though I wouldn't want to trade many of these innovations (Oh, how I love you internet, airplanes, dentistry, and plumbing!), we've lost too much in the dash toward progress. Reaching up to the stars without remembering that we need solid ground beneath our feet sets up every structure and system to fall.

Sovereignty is a human construct—all power plays and nation states and personal psychology. But it's more than that. Sovereignty is rooted into the earth and directly sourced by a connection to Spirit and a sense of a Greater Reality. Always about more than what's going on inside your head, the Sovereignty Knot doesn't just describe the movement from princess to wise woman to queen. It also describes the way we're constantly asked to move from personal concerns to common concerns, from a focus on the environment to a focus on society, from quiet prayer to conscious action. Here we are—just as we should be—back in that infinity loop, recognizing that everything is connected. Here I am realizing that I still get tangled up when I try to integrate my private, inner life with the noisy bitterness of modern culture. I'm accepting my own invitation to do this Sovereignty work so I can pay attention to the state of the world, maintain control of the narrative inside my head, and become a more conscientious, compassionate driver, too.

A conversation about ending our abusive relationship with nature is also about our desire to heal abusive human relationships at every level. Environmental work is social justice work. The fights to stop global warming, dismantle the patriarchy, and end white supremacy are all part of the same evolutionary movement and they are all examples of soul-deep Sovereignty work we must do on behalf of the individual and the collective. Domestic violence prevention, reproductive freedom, LGBTQ rights, the way black and brown people are treated in this world: Whatever your passions, whatever your greatest area of concern, whatever particular cause lifts you out of your everyday obligation, you must choose a patch of earth to stand on and a particular cause to stand for.

You always have choices. Drown in the sea of denial, wither into a swoon of hypocrisy, or step into the maddening modern contradictions with eyes wide open. Even though I know I can lose myself in the chaos of media overload and personal overwhelm, I choose to remain open and conscious as I find myself in yet another iteration of the Sovereignty Knot. Since you've made it all the way through this book, I think it's likely you're making this choice, too. Like me, you've felt the weight of denial and you know the sting of hypocrisy when you offer your support on social media, and then stop there. You know that closing your eyes to certain realities just leads to further unconsciousness—as well as more addiction, consumption, and stress. Maybe you're like me, acknowledging the thrum of worry that this life is not sustainable, this earth cannot bear such treatment, that this way of organizing the global society is unfair. Maybe you, too, want to get free of these lagging fears and be part of the change. Let's trust ourselves and believe we have the power and the presence to engage with the problems of the world without losing ourselves in the mess.

Think of that vision of the Sovereignty Goddess in the cave once more. She understood the abilities and fears of each warrior, artist, and healer who came before her, helped them feel seen and whole, and then she conveyed the gift of Sovereignty to each of them. Next, it was up to them to venture forth to protect, to inspire, and to heal the wider world. When you stand Sovereign in your own body and your own soul, then you have the strength and vision to reach out to tend the earth and all the living creatures that walk, swim, slither, and grow upon it. Empowered by your own sense of agency, ability, and worth, you empower others to claim their own gifts for themselves. As that energy ripples forth, society evolves.

Writing Prompt: The "Why" of Your Sovereignty

In Chapter 1, we explored the "why" of Sovereignty. Here's why I suggest you would want to engage in this quest for Sovereignty:

- to fully inhabit your power, your magic, and your self-worth
- to transform your relationship to age and time
- to use your own growing power to empower others

Now, it's time get the heart of your own reasons for bringing Sovereign energy into your own life. You have met the princess, the queen, and the wise woman. You've had a chance to consider your own stories of Sovereignty. We've explored grief, work, marriage, motherhood, politics, oppression, and our relationship with the environment.

When you look at your own story and then at the wide world with all of its suffering, inequity, and pollution, what strikes you as most relevant and compelling? What needs to be healed? What inspires you to turn your thoughts and prayers into conscious action? Why are you called to stand Sovereign in your own reality?

CHAPTER 12

Experiments in Sovereignty

*T*wo goddesses walk into a bar. One is cloaked in sunlight. The other in moon.

(No, this isn't a joke. It's a story. And as Elizabeth Cunningham's heroine Maeve, the Celtic Mary Magdalen, has taught us, "A story is true if it's well told." I can only pray I can do these immortal women justice...)

One is a darling of the church and a patroness to the pagans, too. The other is slightly more obscure, but she's every bit as powerful and Sovereign.

One is the keeper of life and truth. The other one is, too.

There is Brigid with the gold-kissed hair. You can call her "Saint Bridget," if you really must. And then we have the woman with the jet-black mane. Many call her the Morrígan, but her friends call her Mór. The Christians never bothered trying to domesticate her… the reason why will be clear shortly.

These two divine beings are amongst the oldest, and many would say, the most powerful Sovereignty Goddesses the Celtic world ever did see, and they're just getting their pints.

Now, you might think that the creature who would someday be known as the abbess of Kildare and was even ordained a bishop despite being a member of the frightening (not frail) sex might sip a nice sherry or perhaps a small glass of white wine.

Not so.

"Barkeep!" Brigid called in a voice that would get the cows in from the far pasture, "A lager. And do tell me it will be crisp and cold. I've had a hell of a day out there in the sun. Hanging my cloak on random beams of light isn't as effortless as I make it look. My sister first, though… Mór? The usual?"

"Ah yes, I know I risk being predictable, but yes, a pint of the black stuff." Mór spoke in the low, rich sort of voice of a being who knows she'll be heard (and obeyed).

And so, the fellow behind the bar set about making sure the dark goddess of death and rebirth, of battle and prophecy had her perfect pour of stout. And then he set a nice cold one before the bright goddess of creativity, milk, childbirth, smithcraft, and, yes, beer and brewing. He watched nervously as they clinked glasses and raised them to their lips. He was about to start whinging that he only pulled the pints and couldn't be held responsible for their quality, but they silenced him with a shared look. These ladies had had quite enough of male fragility and all the bloody male domination of the last several millennia and they would be quite content to take it out on the first man who gave them an excuse. He muttered about tending to some business in the back and disappeared from the room. The goddesses continued as if he hadn't been there at all.

"Have you seen the news?" asks Brigid.

Mór cocks an eyebrow and looks at her companion over the rim of her glass. "Oh, come on, I thought we were going to have a nice drink and a chat. You know me and the news these days."

Laughing, Brigid says, "Yes, yes, you were making news before they had paper to print it on. I was, too. But there's something happening over there."

"It's not on the Twitter, is it? I will not engage in a conversation about mortals if we have to discuss the Twitter. To think they consider that a worthy place to wage battle…"

"Not for you, oh Mother of the Battlefield, oh mistress of the raven and the crow!"

Mór fixed Brigid with the stare that melted flesh from the bones of warriors. Brigid grinned back with the confidence of a divine creature who could carry the cornerstone of a cathedral over her arm, and dove back into the question at hand. "No," said Brigid, "This has nothing to do with those silly glowing squares these people need to divine the future. As if looking up to the sky or staring into the flames wasn't good enough for them…" She snorted and shook herself before she embarked on a fresh rant. "No, there's something going on with the women. They're holding their heads higher. They're remembering different stories. The words are taking new shape on their tongues."

"Is it what we've been waiting so long for, sister?" asked Mór, finally dropping her armor enough to look interested.

"Dare say, it is…"

"Are they saying the word?"

Brigid nodded.

"Wait… We've been waiting so long. Which word? Goddess?"

"They have a good hold of that one. It's on T-shirts and things."

"Feminism?"

"Oh they scrawl that across their breasts, too. But they still have that double bind… when they speak up and act out and stop trying to be so pleasant about their revolutionary politics, the mob gets all agitated and starts worrying about what they insist on calling the 'f word.'"

"Oh, for fuck's sake. It must be orgasm, then? Have they finally copped on that the goddesses gave them feminism—and the clitoris, for that matter—because we need them to know pleasure?"

"Turns out they found a way to commodify the orgasm, so they're covered in that department. Some of the little toys they've devised are quite ingenious."

"What, then?" growled Mór. "If you say it fast enough, is 'My eyes are up here, you fucker?' a word?"

"Oh you make me laugh, beloved. As long as women have teets and men have eyes, the girls have been using that phrase. Come on. This is all good fun, but I worry you are being deliberately obtuse."

"Sweet breath of thunder... Have they got it sorted, finally? Did they remember how to ask the question and answer it themselves?"

"Indeed they have, mavourneen."

"What do women want...?" Mór trailed off in a whisper of ecstasy.

They held their glasses in the air, a last great gulp left at the bottom of each. They crashed them together, and before they downed their drinks, they sighed together: "Sovereignty."

"Asked and answered in the same breath now by a growing circle of women."

"Will they forget, do you think?" asked Mór.

"Of course they will. These are human women, after all. They've got jobs and babies and lovers and stacks of books to read. They still have to grind through the jaws of the patriarchy each day—just like we did in our last days on earth. Their world is still built for the forgetting and the oblivion and the suffering, but I have a feeling about this crowd. I have a feeling..."

"Tell me, Brigid, what makes them different?"

"They're not just looking for the crown. And they want more than to just get by. These women are looking for more than a good time— though damn, they are enjoying themselves when they have a chance. They're not going to be satisfied just to say their little prayers and to tuck into their cozy little lives. They're not just in it for themselves or for the tribe that made them. They're looking at each other, as well as the earth and the sky. They're looking for more."

The dark goddess pushed her curls from her forehead and offered a crooked smile. "I see what you did there. Of course they are. I might even make it a bit easier for them to find me now. Now tell me, these are the women we've been waiting for then? They can dance in the dark?"

"The wise ones prefer your territory, sister. They believe in the unseen places where all things begin and end. And they know they can always carry a torch that makes it easy to see the truest shadows. But here you are asking me all the questions as if you didn't prophesize this all on your own."

"Oh, but Brigid, I like it when you tell it in your own sweet way. I have sensed these world changers have been flying in on a new wind. It's blowing fresh seeds to ancient ground."

"Everything is becoming real to them now. Never have they needed it more or been more ready. All that freedom and innovation. All that distraction and suffering. They're learning to live their lives according to Sovereign Time. They're figuring out forgiveness, celebration, gratitude, desire, mortality, and eternity, too."

Just then, a great gale blew the door open. Brigid and Mór's eyes narrowed, offended by the interruption, but then a look of reverence came over them both. One head so fair, one head so dark, they bent for a moment as a silver mist seemed to take over the pub.

"Oh, stop being so pious, sisters. For the love of all things green and growing, aren't we all equal in the eyes of Mother Earth? Who's going to sidle behind there to grab me a nip of whiskey?"

It was, of course, the Cailleach, the wisest and the oldest of the goddesses, the creator of the land itself, the most Sovereign of otherworldly women.

"By my breasts, stop looking so guilty! You deserve to be proud of yourselves and the work you've done. Don't go losing track of your own Sovereignty just because some other Sovereign soul walks into a room. You know better than to let go of your own magic just because a different wind of knowledge and experience comes blowing through a place. You're wiser than that. Start acting that way!"

And so, both Brigid and Mór got up from their stools. Mór climbed to the highest shelf for the twenty-five-year-old gold. Brigid pulled pints like the pro she was. "Sláinte!" they roared, and clinked their glasses with such force that it was clear the vessels themselves were divine.

Smacking her lips, the Cailleach declared: "The quest, my sisters, is to assure these worldly women that the work they've been doing, all this dreaming and remembering and imagining another way, is a truth they can live. They need to know—in their cells, in their souls—that what they know and need is as real as the money in the bank and the hungry mouths at home. As real as the rings on their fingers or the divorce papers in the drawers or the stone in the churchyard. As real as the tribe who lived on their lands before their great-grandmothers were born and the people who live round the block now. As real as the halls of power where the decisions get made. It's their task to do, but it's our privilege to walk beside them."

The two younger goddesses immediately knew what their great gray companion was talking about.

Brigid nodded. "Ritual."

Mór nodded. "Oracle."

Cailleach grinned. "Mineral."

They crashed their glasses together once more. "Sláinte!"

To your good health, my Sovereign Sisters. Cheers.

Ritual, Oracle, Mineral: Exercises and Experiments in Sovereignty

The Sovereignty Knot is a blessing, but it is also a tangle. To recognize these threads within is to begin to see life in an entirely new way. When you can feel your princess voice rising when you actually need the calm of the wise woman to rule the day, you can adjust your approach and speak from a sense of stillness rather than reactivity. When you know your queen is in overdrive, pushing herself and everyone around her to some impossible state of perfection, you can temper her with the lightness of the princess and the unconstrained laughter of the wise woman. For every imbalance, there is a Sovereign remedy.

And yet, it's not as simple as reading about these archetypes and going back to your regularly scheduled stress and distraction. Instead, we look to the Sovereignty Goddesses who know the tides of human nature and Mother Nature, and follow their guidance. *Ritual is the doing. Oracle is the knowing. Mineral is the being.* All of these practices help you to slow down and see how the light and the shadow of each archetype are at play in your life. Ritual, oracle, and mineral open you to consciously move through the points of the Sovereignty Knot. These practices help you lean into the energy of princess, queen, and wise woman when appropriate and offer healing to these parts of your yourself when they've run themselves ragged or feel ignored.

Ritual: The Doing

Ritual is one of those delightful words that you just want to savor on the tongue, but as is so often the case, the dictionary hands us a sanitized set of buttoned-up meanings that have little to do with the messy wonder of feminine life. The *Oxford English Dictionary* tells us that ritual is a "solemn ceremony consisting of a series of actions performed according to a prescribed order," especially one characteristic of a particular religion or church. They give us a dash of the secular, too, and say that it's "a series of actions or type of behavior regularly and invariably followed by someone."

I've spent much of life trying to escape the prescribed order of things (and sometimes I have succeeded). I have also spent that same period creating little rituals, both the daily and the seasonal kind. Ritual helps me step out of the perpetual busyness of the day and into a more sacred, intentional sort of *doing* so I can move consciously through the Sovereignty Knot. We're called to liberate ritual from the temples and the restrictive routines so it looks and feels like something we long to live. What if ritual could be:

- A spiritual or joy-drenched ceremony consisting of a series of actions performed according to intuitive knowing and deep experience.
- The free-flowing engagement in magic, especially one characteristic of the unbridled divine feminine.
- A series of actions regularly and invariably enjoyed by a woman who lives a life of Sovereignty marked by self-love and selfless service.

As much as I want to free us from the formal museum piece of a definition for "ritual," the *regularly* aspect really is non-negotiable. You're called to make a deep, lasting commitment to your own Sovereignty, and you need to show up for yourself day in and day out to make that happen. Your Sovereignty depends on a daily practice that really sets your mind, heart, body, and spirit ablaze—or at least makes you feel fully engaged.

For some, it's a morning meditation. Others connect to Julia Cameron's daily writing routine called Morning Pages. The early parts of the day rarely belong to the mothers amongst us, so it becomes a bedtime ritual, or fifteen minutes stolen over a cup of afternoon tea. Maybe it's your evening run or your after-work yoga class. It could be dancing around your kitchen as you boil pasta. It may be something you're already doing, but you just need to reframe as a beautiful, necessary, Sovereign act. Perhaps you need to create a new habit and install a new ritual into your life. If you're seeking to create a more body-focused set of rituals, you might also enjoy Twyla Tharp's *The Creative Habit*.

You may learn, as I did, that all the things that *don't* work are what will eventually lead you exactly where you need to be. Sitting on a meditation cushion with eyes shut in order to pause and clear the mind is a powerful practice. You're training the brain so, as my coach and meditation teacher Kristoffer "KC" Carter says, you can get your own attention and then direct your own attention for your own highest good. That said, it's still not my Sovereign medicine of choice. Moving my body in yoga practice, writing, getting outside don't necessarily do it, either. Don't get me wrong, I love all of these activities and they're intimately tied to who I am, but they're often too laden with shoulds and obligations. Too often they feel like work, performance, or mere exercise rather than soul food. I need to synthesize these practices and make them my own in order to find myself on my own quest for Sovereignty.

For me, the most meaningful Sovereignty rituals are performed in front of the sprawling altar that has taken over an entire corner of my home office. I'm guided by intuition to create my own practices, integrating meditation, prayer, creativity, movement, and song as the spirit moves me. I often rely on an approach to healing and awakening called Chumpi Illumination. This work was channeled and formalized by my longtime teacher at the Sacred Center Mystery School, Eleanora Amendolara. Incorporating principles of sacred geometry and the Chumpi stones of Peru, CHILL brings together a full spectrum of spiritual traditions and teachings, from the Indian sages to the Native American medicine people to the European alchemists.

Perhaps these practices seem far removed from my own roots in Celtic spirituality, but the truth is found in the eclecticism. As twenty-first century westerners, we've been uprooted from just about all of our shamanic, close-to-the-earth-and-cosmos spiritual practices that helped our ancestors find their way home. We are a blend of cultures and influences, and so are our rituals. In a sacred space filled with stones and statues, Mother Mary sits beside Ganesha and a photo of my mom jumping on a trampoline. This is where I can dream and write and find stillness in my own center.

There's a risk for those of us who have left the religions that shaped the lives of our immediate ancestors. It's possible to become a sort of spiritual tourist who appropriates traditions and faiths, mixing and diluting things in a damaging, disrespectful way. When you seek to create rituals of Sovereignty, ask your wise woman to lead the way. She'll move with sensitivity and discernment, acting as if she has all the time in the world, even though she's the one who best understands mortality and the fleeting nature of time. She'll guide you to a truth that is at once individual and universal.

Writing Prompt: A Review of Your Rituals

When someone recommends you add more conscious habits and rituals to your life, you may be excited to add something magical and new to your routine. Wonderful! Capture that excitement and write down your new ideas. Just remember that imagining a new set of body and soul nourishing rituals isn't the same as *doing* them.

On the other hand, you might be rolling your eyes at the thought of fitting one more thing onto your endless to-do list. The overcommitted queen in me sees the overcommitted queen in you, but then I offer you another idea. Look at your day, your week, your moon cycle, your season, and look at *everything you're already doing.* Take the time to notice the ways you have solid routines that support your Sovereignty. And then, after you've celebrated all that you accomplish all the time, take the time to consider how you can bring more spirit, joy, and magic to the process.

Oracle: The Knowing

My altar space always includes another essential element: a tarot deck. Actually, I have half a dozen oracle decks nearby. I'm not looking for the cards to tell me my future and I'm not sacrificing my agency to chance. Instead, I use the cards to help me slow down and see my situation from a fresh perspective, using the symbols, archetypes, and stories to understand my own situation in a different context. When you're wrestling with a question or a problem, tarot cards can free your typical internal narrative and loosen your grip on "the way it has always been" and "the way it should be." Tarot is one of many ways to gain knowledge along your path to Sovereignty; you might be drawn to a different type of oracle deck, runes, or the *I Ching*. As with ritual, ask yourself what methodology or approach resonates with you.

A tarot deck is a handful of seventy-eight different stories, but really, the possibilities are infinite. Each card has its traditional meaning, and modern decks also layer in the interpretation of their creators. Then, there are all of the shadows and light and nuance you'll bring to every reading, whether it's a formal Celtic Cross spread or simply selecting one card to help you gather your thoughts each day.

I've created a specific Sovereignty Spread that helps you see your own journey with fresh eyes. You can try this with a tarot deck or any oracle deck that assigns specific meanings and qualities to each card.

When I teach and work with individual clients, I introduce the seven aspects of Sovereignty: soul and spirit; partnership and love; work and livelihood; family and caregiving; body and self-care; service and activism; and art and creativity. All of these aspects matter, though some will be particularly important to you and some will be emphasized more than others depending on the season of life. One of the best ways to get familiar with your relationship with each aspect of Sovereignty (because each one can seem too vast to get your mind around at first) is to find guidance in a deck of cards. The Sovereignty Spread works whether you're new to oracle cards or whether you're old friends with the tarot. I have been working with the *Celtic Wisdom Tarot* authored by Caitlin Matthews and illustrated by Olivia Rayner since 1999, but sadly, it's now out of print.

Each card in this eight-card Sovereignty Spread represents a different aspect of Sovereignty. Rather than simply placing card one in the center and setting the rest in a simple circle around it, you're invited to imagine you're drawing a seven-pointed Celtic knot. Follow the diagram's pattern, crisscrossing over the figure to create a seven-pointed star.

The Sovereignty Spread

1. **You:** This card sits at the center of the spread and represents you as you are in relationship to your own personal power and Sovereignty.
2. **Soul and spirit:** This card is placed at the top of the Sovereignty Spread because soul and spirit play a key role in your quest. Yes, this Sovereignty work is about personal agency and self-reliance, but it's always informed by something greater than you. However you understand the divine, ask this card to help you understand your relationship with the unseen world.

3. **Body and self-care:** This card calls you to look at your physical health and your relationship with your body. Past trauma, your relationship to food, drink, and other substances, and body image issues may all come on your quest for Sovereignty. Use this card to compassionately consider how you're treating your body and how you're offering yourself love, nurturing, and forgiveness.

4. **Partnership and love:** This card can refer to a romantic relationship or to other close connections in your life. Because Sovereignty isn't about going it alone, your Sovereignty depends on being in relationships that support your happiness and development. Use this card to focus in on the health of your current primary relationship, to learn what to release, or to determine what to look for if it's time to find someone new.

5. **Work and livelihood:** This card helps you get clear on the role of money and material security in your Sovereignty story. This card can help you consider your relationship with scarcity, abundance, and "enoughness" and determine whether the effort you put forth matches the rewards you receive.

6. **Family and caregiving:** This card can help you get clear on your current role as a parent, a child, a sister, or in any relationship in which you are giving or receiving care. With the help of this card, you can take stock of imbalances and resentments as well as connection and joy.

7. **Service and activism:** This card is most closely related to your relationship with the outer world. Are you putting the right amount of energy into working for the greater good? Use this card to ask yourself whether

you're aligning your values, your skills, and your resources in order to care for this world you love.

8. **Art and creativity:** This card asks you to consider how you're expressing your creative energy and how it might be stagnant or feel actively blocked. Everyone is an artist in their way, whether that ever shows up on the page, on the stage, in the kitchen, or in the bedroom. Use this card to ask yourself how you're drawn to make conscious creativity a part of your Sovereignty journey.

Writing Prompt: What the Oracle Says

There's an excellent chance you have an oracle deck in your possession. You might have a tarot deck or some other tool for divination. If you don't have one, take yourself out for a Sovereign splurge and purchase cards or some other oracular tool that speaks to your heart. My favorite decks (listed in the resources section) are related to Celtic mythology and goddesses from around the world, and tend to tell a story on each card.

Sit down and try the Sovereignty Spread to get some insight into the aspects of Sovereignty listed above. Write into what you discover. Let yourself linger as each card may open up a whole new world of insight and symbol.

Mineral: The Being

The final word belongs to the Cailleach, the divine being who shaped the earth, especially the cliffs and the caves. It is her voice that speaks through you when you have the courage to say (and believe) what all Sovereignty Goddesses know: "It all comes back to the land."

It's easy to forget about the earth as we speak of princesses and their checkered pasts, and queens all safe in their castles. This work of becoming human is heady, civilized stuff and it isolates us from the natural world. As human creatures, we can attune ourselves to the crash of waves, the crunch of gravel, the shadows cast by a full autumn moon. We can translate the huff of the deer, the creak of naked boughs, and the silence of growing things, and to turn them into meaning. We can catch the whispers of wind and trust that all of these elementals are worthy of our attention. We can. But so often, we don't. There are bills to pay, old traumas to heal, kids to feed, a lover to kiss. The radio is on and the Amazon is burning and the Amazon delivery is late, but it feels there's nothing you can do but worry, drink coffee, and read the next article in the digital stream.

Through the Sovereignty Knot, we remember. Through the deities, the stories, the land itself, and the power rising within, we tune back in. We hear a voice as ancient as the stones. It's a voice that lilts like falling rain and booms like a flooded stream. Hear this voice, anchor into the patch of earth upon which you stand, and know what it is to be home. And when you enter into such a communion, you can find your truth and your Sovereignty, at any place and at any time. To engage in this wordless conversation with the earth herself is the furthest thing from tuning out or hiding away. Quite the contrary, this sense of being in nature, in being with your *own* nature is everything. Without a relationship to the land, all the rituals, all the oracles, and all the talk of crowns and human freedom is like dancing to a broken melody or being a singer without a song.

This book started with a journey into an Irish cave, at the edge of the otherworld that exists before life and after death. You don't need to begin with a peak experience (or a depth experience, either) to fill your Sovereignty Map with meaning. As part of your quest for Sovereignty, you may choose to unfurl a huge piece of fresh paper and begin to draw your map, populating it with your experiences and landmarks that help you find your way around your imaginal world. You may also wish to pull out a real map of your local area and get to know its topography. Seek out the names of the mountains and rivers in the words the native people used, particularly if you live in a part of the world that was colonized and taken from its indigenous inhabitants. As you develop a relationship with the land beneath your feet, you also cultivate a sense of gratitude for the people who came before and lived in harmony with this land.

True and lasting Sovereignty is rooted in the work you do at this moment. No matter where you are, in a desert of groomed grass or within a well-paved grid, nature wants to greet you, hold you, partner with you. This is true of Sovereignty, too. Wherever you are in your life, the princess, queen, and wise woman want to flow within you and help move you along.

Pause now. Summon the courage to be with the noise of the endless crickets or the stillness of the frost. Allow the rush of the traffic and the rumble of the furnace, too. Our work is to stand Sovereign in reality, not in idealized dreams. There is a voice that entwines above and below it all, echoing at every register through every corner of the world. This voice is present in every cell and every thought, everything that happened and might have been, every moment as it flows and every possibility beyond.

This voice is yours. It is the sound of your princess, your queen, and your wise woman coming together as one. Lift this voice to sing the song of an artist, a sorceress, a warrior. Raise your voice to heal, to teach, to change this terribly gorgeous tangle of a world.

Welcome. *Fáilte.* You've come so far. Your adventure has just begun.

Writing Prompt: First, Go Outside

In the ideal world, you'd be able to pick up your journal and a pen and you would walk out the door and find a comfy seat and start telling the story of the natural world that surrounds you.

I'm hoping you can make that happen, but since we are dealing with the world as it is and working the practical side of magic here, we need to acknowledge that it just might be midnight and twelve degrees below zero where you are right now. If weather or circumstance is keeping you locked up indoors and it's impossible for you to take your writing practice outside, please seek out another way to bring the outside environment into your daily ritual and to the page.

Tell the story of the cold wind, the bleak colors, the bitter chill. Tell the story of the air that tastes like exhaust and the endless sound of traffic that's always louder than the birds. Be with these sensory experiences, as well as the emotions they evoke.

There will be days when you can tell stories of gentle air, cerulean skies, and soft grass. You will be somewhere where the breeze tastes like ocean sweetness or crisp autumn purity and all you hear is the call of the wood thrush. When you've primed your senses on the bleakest days, you'll be all the more receptive to beauty.

Describe what's true and open yourself to what might be possible.

Writing Prompt: Your Own Definition of Sovereignty

You've spiraled through the Sovereignty Knot with me and you've explored the "why" behind your Sovereignty.

Now, it's about the *being* of Sovereignty. What does it look, sound, taste, smell, and feel like?

Start with a fresh page and write at the top in great, bold letters **When I am Sovereign, I am...** Keep writing until there are no words left to say. Then trust that the next time you work with this prompt you'll be at a new point in the Sovereignty Knot and you'll have even more stories to tell and insights to explore.

Resources

WORKS CITED

Armstrong, Karen. *A Short History of Myth*. Edinburgh: Canongate, 2005.

Blackie, Sharon. *If Women Rose Rooted*. Tewkesbury, England: September Publishing, 2016.

Condren, Mary. *The Serpent and the Goddess*. San Francisco: Harper & Row, 1989.

Dalai Lama, His Holiness the. *Mind of Clear Light: Advice on Dying and Living a Better Life*. New York: Atria Books, 2003.

Goldberg, Natalie. *Writing Down the Bones*. Boston: Shambhala, 1986.

Gwynn, Edward, trans. *The Metrical Dindshenchas*. Revised Feb 3, 2011. **https://celt.ucc.ie/published/T106500D.html.**

Kristeva, Julia. *The Kristeva Reader*. Edited by Toril Moi. New York: Columbia University Press, 1986. pp. 187–213.

Meehan, Paula. *Pillow Talk*. Loughcrew, Ireland: Gallery Press, 1994. p. 50.

Ní Dhomhnaill, Nuala. *Selected Poems: Rogha Dánta*. Dublin: New Island Books, 2000.

Ó Crualaoich, Gearoid. *The Book of the Cailleach*. Cork: Cork University Press, 2003.

Ó hAodha, Donnchadh, trans. *Bethu Brigte*. Revised Sept 7, 2008. **https://www.ucc.ie/celt/published/T201002/index.html**.

Starhawk. *Truth or Dare: Encounters with Power, Authority, and Mystery*. San Francisco: Harper Collins, 1987.

Stokes, Whitley, trans. *On the Life of St. Brigit*. Revised June 14, 2013. **https://celt.ucc.ie//published/T201010/index.html**.

Winterson, Jeanette. *The PowerBook*. New York: Alfred A. Knopf, 2001. p. 203.

INFLUENTIAL TEACHERS
& THINKERS

Eleanora Amendolara, www.sacredcenter.net: creator of Chumpi Illumination energy healing and founder of the Sacred Center Mystery School. (See also: Chumpi Illumination: Gateways to Healing and Transformation by Eleanora Amendolara with Marisa Goudy, Portland, Oregon: Devera Publishing, 2014.)

Elizabeth Cunningham, www.elizabethcunninghamwrites.com: author of many novels and books of poetry including The Maeve Chronicles, a four-book series: *Magdalen Rising: The Beginning, The Passion of Mary Magdalen, Bright Dark Madonna,* and *Red-Robed Priestess.*

Kristoffer "KC" Carter, www.thisepiclife.com: a coach and spiritual teacher who offers powerful meditation and mindset tools.

OTHER RESOURCES

Podcast

Thin Places Podcast: https://thinplacespodcast.com/. For more on Oweynagat: https://thinplacespodcast.com/ep3-rathcroghan-people-of-the-mounds/.

Books

Julia Cameron. *The Artist's Way.* New York: Penguin, 2016.

Ciaran Carson. *The Táin.* New York: Penguin Classics, 2008.

Twyla Tharp, *The Creative Habit: Learn It and Use It for Life.* New York: Simon & Schuster, 2003.

Tarot Decks

Anna-Marie Ferguson. *Legend: The Arthurian Tarot.* Woodbury, MN: Llewellyn Worldwide, 1996.

Sage Holloway. *Mythical Goddess Tarot.* Artist, Katherine Skaggs. Fort Collins, CO: Star Chalice Sisters Publishing, 2015.

Caitlín Matthews. *Celtic Wisdom Tarot.* Artist, Olivia Rayner. New York: HarperCollins, 1999.

ABOUT THE AUTHOR

Marisa Goudy is a writer who offers writing coaching and energy healing to clients around the world. She is the founder of The Sovereign Writers Circle, the online community for healers who write and writers who heal.

Marisa holds a bachelor's degree from Boston College and a master's degree in Anglo-Irish Literature and Drama from University College Dublin and continues to study modern Irish women's poetry, Irish myth, and Celtic spirituality. Marisa has co-written the book *Chumpi Illumination: Gateways to Healing and Transformation* with her Sacred Center Mystery School teacher Eleanora Amendolara.

Originally from Cape Cod, Massachusetts, Marisa spent time in Ireland before moving to New York's Hudson Valley, where she now lives with her husband, daughters, and cats named Big Love MacLir and Little Dude McCool.

To learn more about Marisa's coaching, healing, and tarot reading services, as well as the Sovereign Writers Circle, the online program Your Sovereign Awakening, and in-person Sovereignty retreats, please visit www.marisagoudy.com.

CPSIA information can be obtained
at www.ICGtesting.com
Printed in the USA
LVHW090218060220
646053LV00001B/115

9 781734 194005